POWER

IN EXPOSITORY
PREACHING

POWER
IN EXPOSITORY
PREACHING

POWER

IN EXPOSITORY
PREACHING

Faris D. Whitesell

FLEMING H. REVELL COMPANY

Preface

EXPOSITORY PREACHING IS THE ideal of most ministers, but relatively few of them would claim real stature as expository preachers. In spite of several books on expository preaching, and frequent magazine articles encouraging it, many pastors hesitate to undertake it seriously; of those who do practice it, most feel that they fall short of doing it well. This book is an attempt not only to stimulate expository preaching, but to portray the true sources of power for it in down-to-earth terms.

During the school year of 1960-61 I had the students in my three preaching classes circulate a one-page questionnaire on expository preaching among their pastor friends. About fifty students participated in the project and 223 questionnaires were filled out and returned. Ministers across the nation returned questionnaires, but most were returned by pastors in the middle west. Theologically the returns came primarily from pastors of the conservative, evangelical persuasion, with a few exceptions. Denominationally there was quite a spread, with Baptist pastors far in the lead—American Baptists, National Baptists, Free Will Baptists, Conservative Baptists, Regular Baptists, Southern Baptists, and Independent Baptists. We also had the cooperation of Methodist, Wesleyan Methodist, Free Methodist, Presbyterian, Pentecostal, Church of God, Evangelical Free, Evangelical United Brethren, Christian and Missionary Alliance pastors. This is a small sampling of the more than 250,000 pastors in our land, to be sure, but it does give us some interesting information.

The first question was: "Do you prefer to preach topically——? Textually——? Expositorially——? (check one)." One hundred and forty pastors checked that they preferred to preach expository sermons; fifty-three textual; and thirty-six topical.

The next question was: "Which method predominates in your preaching: Topical——? Textual——? Expository——? (check one)." In answer to this question, one hundred checked expository, seventy-nine textual, and thirty-six topical. Evidently more men prefer to preach expository sermons than actually do. I suspect that the percentage who checked expository as their predominant method runs much higher than that of the Protestant ministry as a whole in America.

The third question concerned the preference of their congregations: "Which method of preaching does your congregation seem to prefer: Topical——? Textual——? Expository——? No preference——? (check one)." This question had to be answered somewhat subjectively and its results are not too valuable, but eighty checked expository, thirty-six topical, thirty-one textual, and fifty-seven no preference. If congregations could hear good expository preaching for a year or more, I have no doubt that a percentage much higher than the twenty-eight shown here would prefer it. Many congregations have wrong ideas about expository preaching.

The questionnaire bore this paragraph at the beginning:

Definitions: For this purpose, *a topical sermon* is built around a subject-idea taken from the Bible or outside of the Bible. A *textual sermon* is one based on a verse or two from the Bible, the main theme and the major sermon divisions coming from the text. An *expository sermon* is based on a Bible passage, usually longer than a verse or two; the theme, the thesis and the major and minor divisions coming from the passage; the whole sermon being an honest attempt to unfold the true grammatical-historical-contextual meaning of the passage, making it relevant to life today by proper organization, argument, illustrations, application and appeal.

These definitions were needed in order to secure intelligent answers to our questions.

In addition to the above positive definition of expository preaching, let us try to define it negatively by indicating what, in my opinion, is *not* expository preaching.

1. It is not running commentary from word to word and verse to verse without unity, outline, and persuasive drive.

2. It is not rambling comment and offhand remarks about the passage apart from thorough exegesis and logical order.

3. It is not a mass of disconnected suggestions and inferences based on the surface meaning of the passage but not sustained by a depth-and-breadth study of the text.

4. It is not pure exegesis, no matter how scholarly, if it lacks theme, thesis, outline and development.

5. It is not a mere structural outline of the passage with a few supporting comments but lacking other rhetorical and sermonic elements.

6. It is not a topical homily using scattered parts of the passage but omitting discussion of other equally important parts.

7. It is not a chopped-up collection of grammatical findings and quotations from commentaries without being fused together into a smooth, flowing, interesting and compelling message.

8. It is not a Sunday school lesson discussion

of a Bible passage organized around a contents outline, informal and fervent, but lacking sermonic structure and rhetorical factors.

9. It is not a Bible reading which links together a number of scattered Bible passages around a common theme but does not deal with any of them in a thorough, grammatical and contextual manner.

10. It is not the ordinary devotional or prayer meeting talk which combines running commentary, rambling remarks, disconnected suggestions, and personal reactions into a semi-inspirational discussion, but without the benefit of basic exegetical-contextual study and the persuasive elements of a sermon.

Let me hasten to say that some, maybe all, of the ten Biblical presentations listed above have some value. Any one of them, or any combination of them, may do much good, particularly when presented by a speaker of spiritual fervor and enthusiasm. In fact, we must use a few of these processes in the preparation of an expository sermon, but emphatically none of them, nor the combination of all of them, can rightly be called an expository sermon.

In order to be fair, I wish to give the ideas of a number of other men about expository preaching. While there is considerable variety, even disagreement, among them, I hope that this review of the concepts of others will help to clarify and solidify our own ideas on this subject.

It is impossible to separate these definitions into classifications in an absolute sense, but in a relative sense it can be done. In spite of considerable overlapping, I have taken one major idea from each man as representative of his concept of expository preaching, and have listed the definitions in five categories.

First, some think of expository preaching as a connected

series of sermons through a book of the Bible. William M. Taylor wrote: "By expository preaching, I mean that method of pulpit discourse which consists in the consecutive interpretation, and practical enforcement of a book of the sacred canon."[1]

F. B. Meyer gave this as his view: "Expository preaching is the consecutive treatment of some book or extended portion of Scripture on which the preacher has concentrated head and heart, brain and brawn, over which he has thought and wept and prayed, until it has yielded up its inner secret, and the spirit of it has passed into his spirit."[2]

Charles R. Brown, in reviewing his preaching for nearly fifteen years in his last church, says: "I preached courses of expository sermons to that one congregation as follows: From the Old Testament, six months on Genesis, three months on Exodus, three months on Joshua, three months on Judges, two months on the life of Elijah as recorded in Kings, two months on Job, six months on Isaiah, two months on the minor prophets. . . . In the New Testament, I preached for six months on Matthew, six months on Mark, twelve months on Luke, which to me is the greatest and dearest book in all the Bible, six months on John, six months on Acts, two months on Romans, three months on first and second Corinthians, and two months on the Book of Revelation."[3]

Second, other men distinguish expository preaching from textual preaching by the fact that it discusses a passage longer than two or three verses. Andrew W. Blackwood writes: "Expository preaching means that the light for any sermon comes mainly from a Bible passage longer than two or three consecutive verses."[4]

Ilion T. Jones thinks of expository preaching as interpreting a chapter, a portion of a chapter or a whole book of the Bible.[5]

Douglas M. White said: "In distinction to both the topical and textual sermon, the expository sermon is a treatment of a single extended passage of Scripture, a lengthy paragraph, a chapter, or more than a chapter, or even a whole book of the Bible."[6]

T. H. Pattison appeared to be in agreement with this idea when he wrote: ". . . the topical sermon, in which the theme is especially prominent; the textual sermon, in which more regard is paid to the words of the text; and the expository sermon, in which, as a rule, a longer portion of the Bible is taken as the basis for the discourse."[7]

Michael Reu gives the expository sermon two major characteristics: "The expository sermon is not really a third genus, but is a species of the analytic sermon, having for its specific purpose the expository treatment of longer passages or of entire books of the Bible. It must not, however, descend, as it is prone to do, to a formless discourse without unity, completeness or logical and rhetorical movement."[8]

Peter T. Forsyth said: "Preach more expository sermons. Take long passages for texts. Perhaps you have no idea how eager people are to have the Bible expounded, and how much they prefer you to unriddle what the Bible says. . . ."[9]

Third, other authorities bear down on the idea that expository preaching is mainly explanation of the Scriptures. John A. Broadus wrote in the first edition of his famous textbook: "An expository discourse may be defined as one which is occupied mainly, or at any rate very largely, with the exposition of Scripture. It by no means excludes argument and exhortation as to the doctrines or lessons which this exposition develops. It may be devoted to a long passage, or a very short one, even a part of a sentence. It may be one of a series, or may stand by itself. We at once perceive that there is no broad line of division between expository preaching and the common methods, but that one may pass by almost insensible gradations from textual to expository sermons."[10]

Austin Phelps treats expository preaching as one type of explanatory preaching. He indicates that if the text is the theme, and if the chief object of the sermon is to explain the text by elaborate treatment with a view to persuasion, it is an expository sermon.[11]

Harry Jeffs wrote: "Exposition is the art of opening up the Scriptures, laying them out, reproducing their matter and their spirit in forms vitalized by the personality of the expositor . . . the main purpose of exposition is to apply the knowledge of Scripture to serviceable uses. The skill is perfected by practice."[12]

R. Ames Montgomery wrote: "The expository preacher purposes above everything else to make clear the teaching and content of the Bible. . . . The preacher seeks to bring the message of definite units of God's Word to his people. He discovers the main theme or constituent parts of a book's message as they were in the mind of the writer. These he unfolds step by step until he reaches the ultimate goal. He discovers the universal, organizing elements of thought in the book, and strives to set forth their essential relationship to contemporary life."[13]

Donald Grey Barnhouse expressed this view: "Expository preaching is the art of explaining the text of the Word of God, using all the experience of life and learning to illuminate the exposition."[14]

Fourth, there are those who believe that the way in which the Bible passage is handled determines whether or not it is an expository sermon. John Hall gave this rather elaborate definition: "By expository preaching we mean that in which a minister, having by the aid of grammar, dictionary, and all proper helps, learns for himself what meaning the Holy Ghost intended to convey in the passage he has in hand, and then what use he ought, in harmony with the rest of divine teaching to make of it, and having filled his own understanding, and warmed his own heart with this truth, tells it to his people with clearness, simplicity, force, and fervor."[15]

David R. Breed set forth this view: "The expository sermon is the product of exegesis, but it is in no sense its exhibition. It is not a running commentary upon some passage of Scripture in which its separate parts are taken up seriatim and explained, but, as its name implies, it is a piece of rhetoric: a sermon. It differs from the topical sermon in that it is all derived directly from the Scripture; and it differs from the textual sermon in that more of the details of the Scripture passage are employed."[16]

Jeff D. Ray claimed that "In preaching, exposition is the detailed interpretation, logical amplification, and the practical application of a passage of Scripture. . . . Exegesis draws out the hidden meaning; exposition places that meaning out in logical, appropriate, effective order. Exegesis is the task of the commentator; exposition is the task of the preacher."[17]

G. Campbell Morgan does not give a true definition of expository preaching as such but probably expresses his idea of it in the following: "Being sure that our text is in the Bible, we proceed to find out its actual meaning, and then to elaborate its message. . . . Elaboration is far more than simple statement. The text has postulates, implicates, deductions, applications. . . . The sermon is the text repeated more fully in that these things—postulates, implicates, deductions, applications—are discovered and declared, or at least recognized."[18]

Merrill F. Unger flatly states: "However if a clear and

unconfused definition is to be arrived at, the valid criterion, it would seem, is not the length of the portion treated, whether a single verse or a larger unit, but the manner of treatment."[19] ". . . expository preaching must be biblical, biblically instructive, challenging, consistent with the whole of biblical truth, and must come to grips with the human will and conscience."[20]

David Martyn Lloyd-Jones, present minister at Westminster Chapel, London, does not consider mere exposition or running commentary expository preaching. He says: ". . . what turns it into preaching is that it becomes a message and that it has a distinct form and pattern . . . it must always be applied and its relevance shown to the contemporary situation."[21]

Fifth, there is the view that any preaching drawn from the Bible is expository preaching. Donald G. Miller contends that all such criteria as length of passage handled, method of analysis, explanatory emphasis, and consecutive handling of a long passage, are beside the point. The true criterion, he insists, is that ". . . the substance of one's preaching should be drawn from the Bible. Granted this premise, then it follows that all true preaching is expository preaching, and that preaching which is not expository is not preaching."[22]

Miller's general view of preaching follows the neo-orthodox pattern which claims that preaching should re-enact the redemptive deeds of God in Christ so that the hearer is confronted with the living Christ in judgment and redemption. This is the view of John Knox and other neo-orthodox leaders.

These views of what expository preaching is should help us to understand it and to distinguish it from the topical and textual methods of preaching. But in order to illustrate what I conceive to be the distinctions between topical, textual, and expository methods, let me use a tree as an example. It is a particular, large oak tree in our front yard. Instead of talking about a passage of Scripture, we shall talk about this tree. The topical approach takes one major part of the tree as the subject of discussion and dismisses the rest of the tree. Suppose we take the trunk of the tree as our subject, then discuss tree trunks—all kinds of tree trunks—their values and uses.

In the textual method, we shall be interested in the whole tree. We divide our message into three parts, according to the three major parts of the tree: the roots, the trunk, and the branches. From the data about our particular tree we make comparisons and contrasts with other trees as to their roots, trunks, and branches.

In the expository approach, we study not only the roots, trunk, and branches of our tree, we also consider its leaves, soil, climate, inner ring system, distinctive features, life history, and relation to other trees and vegetation around it; the uses to which we can put this tree, and how to reproduce this tree and others like it not only here but in other parts of the world. In other words, we seek a comprehensive, detailed, and thorough knowledge of our tree. From the mass of information which we compile, we arrange our expository talk about our tree. We find a subject, a theme, a thesis, a logical outline, and a sound development. We may not use all of the material we have gathered, but we use most of it. This is the expository method.

Perhaps you are saying, "What difference does it make how all these men define expository preaching? Isn't the main thing to do it? Can't a person do it in his own way without troubling about definitions and distinctions?" Yes, the main thing is to do it, but how can one do something unless he knows what he is trying to do?

Or, maybe you are saying, "I'm more confused than helped by all these definitions. After all, please tell me exactly what expository preaching is." All I can do is to give my own conception of it. I believe that it involves a number of factors:

1. It is based on a passage in the Bible, either short or long.

2. It seeks to learn the primary, basic meaning of that passage.

3. It relates that meaning to the context of the passage.

4. It digs down for the timeless, universal truths stemming out of the passage.

5. It organizes these truths tightly around one central theme.

6. It uses the rhetorical elements of explanation, argument, illustration, and application to bring the truth of the passage home to the hearer.

7. It seeks to persuade the listener to obey the truth of the passage discussed.

My view is in line with the fourth class of definitions given—that expository preaching depends on the way the passage is handled, rather than its length or its contents. I believe that most of us would do better to preach on big passages of Scripture rather than small ones. Let us give the people the Bible in big chunks rather than in tiny portions. We are more likely to stay on the track of the Word of God if we do.

By now you may be asking, "But is there anything wrong with topical and textual preaching? Aren't these valid methods?" Yes, indeed they are. I accept them both. If one wishes to preach on a broad, general theme, as is often the case in doctrinal preaching, the topical method is the one to use. Or, if some verse calls for discussion, the textual method might be the one to use, but I am of the opinion that the expository approach should be the main one for pastoral preaching. It settles more preaching problems than any other, and does more good for pastor and people alike.

Again, you may ask, "But is expository preaching really better? Doesn't it depend on what is natural and easy to the individual preacher?" No, the natural and easy way may not be better. I am convinced that the expository method is really better, and hope to demonstrate this in the pages ahead.

Finally, you may inquire, "Isn't expository preaching much harder? Doesn't it take more time to prepare, and isn't it more difficult to make interesting?" Yes, to all three questions. But what is the test of how we should serve God? Is it the measure of difficulty involved in a task? The criterion should be, What will do the most good for the most people over the longest period of time, and thus bring most glory to God? Expository rates first by this test. Any type of preaching should require hard work. Expository preaching probably requires no more work than any other type, once a preacher gets into the habit of doing it. This we hope to show. From here on we are to think of the avenues of power open to the expository preacher.

Faris D. Whitesell

Contents

Contents

I
Power Through
MOTIVATION

WHY ARE THERE NOT more consistent, first-rate expository preachers? The answer might be that not enough men have the motivation to achieve proficiency in this field. We need adequate motivation to accomplish anything worthwhile. This chapter is devoted to consideration of the motives which should spur preachers into a ministry of expository preaching.

A review of one's call and commission into the Christian ministry should focus attention on the responsibility to preach the Word of God. The Bible is to be our textbook and guide. It should be the source of preaching ideas and pulpit authority. Jesus commanded Peter, "Feed my lambs. . . . Tend my sheep " (John 21:15-17, RSV); and Paul exhorted the Ephesian elders "to feed the church of the Lord which he obtained with his own blood" (Acts 20:28, RSV). The best way to feed the children of God is to preach the Bible in big portions. Paul probably had this same work in mind when he wrote to Timothy, ". . . preach the word, be urgent in season and out of season, convince, rebuke and exhort, be unfailing in patience and in teaching" (II Timothy 4:2, RSV).

God calls men into the ministry to preach His Word, not their own ideas or the current trends in human thought. A congregation can learn what men think through their newspapers, magazines, and other news media, but the question is: What does God think and say? William M. Taylor was right when he said: "You are to be ministers of the Word: and it is by the knowledge of the Scriptures that you are to be thoroughly furnished for your work. The Bible is your textbook, and that not in the sense of being a hunting-ground for texts, but in that of constituting the groundwork of your discourses."[1]

And, was Harry Jeffs of England too radical when he wrote: "The Bible is the preacher's Book and the preacher's glory. Bible exposition is the preacher's main business. If he cannot or will not expound the Bible, what right has he in any pulpit? He is a cumberer of the ground, and worse than a cumberer, for he is occupying uselessly ground that might be occupied by a fruit-bearing and soul-nourishing tree. If he does not expound the Bible what else is there for him to do? He may deliver addresses 'out of his own head' on any subject that occurs to him, and may do it very well, but why do it in a pulpit?"[2]

If the preacher reviews his call and commission, but finds that his confidence in the power and authority of the Scriptures has been shattered, what can he do? Occasionally ministers do have this problem and they have our sympathy. Maybe they have studied under critical scholars, or have read too deeply in modern philosophy and theology, or have gone through bitter experiences in life. They do not, and say they cannot, hold orthodox views of the Bible. But they can try. G. Campbell Morgan, one of the world's greatest expository preachers, had such an experience in his early days. His daughter-in-law writes:

At last the crisis came when he admitted to himself his total lack of assurance that the Bible was the authoritative Word of God to man. He immediately cancelled all preaching engage-

2

ments. Then, taking all his books, both those attacking and those defending the Bible, he put them all in a corner cupboard. Relating this afterwards, as he did many times in preaching, he told of turning the key in the lock of the door. "I can hear the click of that lock now," he used to say. He went out of the house, and down the street to a bookshop. He bought a new Bible and, returning to his room with it, he said to himself: "I am no longer sure that this is what my father claims it to be—the Word of God. But of this I am sure. If it be the Word of God, and if I come to it with an unprejudiced and open mind, it will bring assurance to my soul of itself. That Bible found me," he said, "I began to read and study it then, in 1883. I have been a student ever since, and I still am (in 1938)."

At the end of two years Campbell Morgan emerged from that eclipse of faith absolutely sure that the Bible was, in very deed and truth, none other than the Word of the living God. . . . With this crisis behind him and this new certainty thrilling his soul, there came a compelling conviction. This Book, being what it was, merited all that a man could give to its study, not merely for the sake of the personal joy of delving deeply into the heart and mind and will of God, but also in order that those truths discovered by such searching of the Scriptures should be made known to a world of men groping for light, and perishing in the darkness with no clear knowledge of that Will.[3]

A similar case closer to our own days is that of Billy Graham, the evangelist. He wrote an article in the October 15, 1956, issue of *Christianity Today*, telling how he came through such a crisis in August, 1949: "I dueled with my doubts, and my soul seemed to be caught in the crossfire. Finally, in desperation, I surrendered my will to the living God revealed in Scripture. I knelt before the open Bible and said, 'Lord, many things in this Book I do not understand. But Thou hast said, "The just shall live by faith." All I have received from Thee, I have taken by faith. Here and now, by faith, I accept the Bible as Thy word. I take

3

it all. I take it without reservations. Where there are things I cannot understand, I will reserve judgment until I receive more light. If this please Thee, give me authority as I proclaim Thy word, and through that authority convict me of sin and turn sinners to the Saviour.' "[4] Soon after that came the Los Angeles Crusade which launched Billy Graham into the field of world evangelism, and ever since he has preached the Word with power.

If a pastor wishes to add depth, dignity, direction, and dynamics to his preaching, let him perfect himself in the expository method. The great expositor, William M. Taylor, insists that the preacher's ". . . special power is that he has God's Word behind him, and if through the neglect of expounding that Word he fails to use this power with effect, he is like Samson shorn of his locks, and will be sure to be made sport of by the Philistines of his generation. Hence, as an engine of power, I advocate most earnestly the systematic pulpit exposition of the sacred Scriptures."[5]

F. B. Meyer claims that the expository preacher has a better chance of appealing successfully to the conscience, and of capturing and compelling the will, because his appeals are based on more Scripture, have a broader basis of truth, and are likely to have more of the empowerment of the Holy Spirit.[6]

The challenge of following in the train of the great exemplars of expository preaching should be some motivation to a preacher. Think of the spirtual help expository preachers have given to others. Men like Matthew Henry, Joseph Parker, Marcus Dods, George Adam Smith, G. Campbell Morgan, Alexander Maclaren, and W. B. Riley helped not only through their pulpit ministry but through their written ministry! Hardly a pastor's library anywhere exists without containing one or more volumes from these men, and when the pastor preaches the Bible, he turns to them for help.

Living preachers are putting their best expository sermons into print and thus are extending and perpetuating their lives' work. Volumes of topical and textual sermons, no matter how popular and how good, soon have done their work and are cast aside. But books of good expository sermons remain in use long after the author has left this world. Expository preachers like Paul S. Rees, Harold J. Ockenga, D. Martyn Lloyd-Jones, Roy Laurin, Alan Redpath, Lehman Strauss, Douglas M. White, and Helmut Thielicke, are producing expository sermon volumes which will be around for a long time. The writer believes that any dedicated preacher can publish at least one book of expositions. He can, if he is willing to write out his sermons in full, revise, rewrite, polish and correct until they meet publishers' standards.

Does the preacher wish to rise above the level of being a sermon mill or homiletical machine grinding out two or three sermons a week? If he will get into the expository habit and fall in line with the great expository preachers, sermon production will be a joy. He will regret that he cannot spend more time in his study preparing sermons, and that he has such a few years left to preach the Bible.

Joseph Parker, after seven years of preaching through much of the Bible, wrote: "I care less and less for mere catch-texts and for small ingenuities in pulpit mechanics. Our cleverness is our destruction as expositors. In its exercise we lose breadth, substance, and dignity, and become mere tricksters and jugglers. I care very little for mere literary polish in preaching. We want intelligence, unction, and directness. All the rest is comparatively worthless. The preacher is not an author reading his own manuscript; he is a voice, a fire, a herald, bold and eager in his sacred work—an orator speaking in Heaven's name and strength."[7]

Are you open for something to renew your ministry? Something to lift you out of the doldrums? Something to make the chores of the ministry take on new importance? Something to thrill you intellectually, emotionally, and spiritually? Something to give you a new grip on the power of God and make you glad you are a preacher? Give expository preaching a realistic trial for a year.

Imagine that you are standing before the judgment seat of Christ. Life's work is all over and every deed, word, attitude, and thought is passing in review before the fiery test of that day. Will you be most glad for your topical preaching? Your textual? Your expository? Which is most likely to be wood, hay, stubble—which gold, silver and precious stone? Which type would equip you with the most spiritual knowledge and discernment for the heavenly life before you?

Parishioners expect their pastor to be a master of the Bible. Will he ever master it unless he lives in it and preaches all through it in sizable portions? The Bible deserves to be explored, tested, verified, mastered and preached. The desire to win the respect and approval of his spiritual members—the Bible-believers and Bible-lovers—should prompt a pastor to specialize in expository preaching. True enough, he is to seek to please God rather than men; but if he has some members with the mind of Christ and love for the Word, is he not pleasing God when he pleases them?

How can the pastor make his immature members Biblically literate and spiritually mature? Nothing will help them more than interesting expository preaching.

Harold J. Ockenga has written: "My own conviction is that we must get back to expository preaching, beginning as did Zwingli, the Swiss reformer, in the first verse of the Book of Matthew and preaching right through the New Testament, so that our congregations may be truly conversant with the doctrines, precepts and practices of New Testament Christianity."[8]

R. Ames Montgomery, discussing the consistent expositor, wrote: "His own congregation will be edified and built up in Christian faith and character. He will gain a reputation for sound and instructive preaching. He will become established in the esteem and affection of his public."[9]

If the pastor seeks to develop a working and witnessing church, he will go a long way toward achieving this goal by preaching expository sermons. Such sermons will show the people the greatness of the Bible and the God of the Bible. They will be equipped to witness and inspired to work. Sunday school teachers will be better prepared to teach. People will be inspired to read their Bibles and to carry them. Is the church too worldly? Expository preaching will feed the saints, wean them from the world and set their affections on things above. Is the stewardship level low in the church? Expository sermons will, in the course of time, cover all the facets of Christian stewardship without singling it out for an over-emphasis. Is there too little soul-winning zeal and missionary concern? Expounding the Scriptures will bring God's answer to these needs. One pastor gives this testimony: "After ten years of topical, textual, doctrinal, and general preaching, I have spent the past three years in expository preaching entirely, with these results: More souls have been saved, more improvements have been made to church properties, and more money has been given to missionary causes than in any other similar period in the church's history; and it was God working through His Word that did it all!"[10]

Bernard Ramm has this to say: "Expository preaching makes for a well-rounded ministry. Some preachers never get away from the Pauline epistles, others are "bugs" on prophetic themes, others have pet doctrinal themes. But

7

an expository preacher, by his very method, is spread all over the Bible. He and his people survey the entire range of divine truth, from Genesis to Revelation. The result is that there is education, edification, and spiritual maturation."[11]

A pastor should plan to preach through the whole Bible in every pastorate. How else can he preach the whole counsel of God in any given place? This would be impossible if the preacher preached paragraph-by-paragraph through each book of the Bible. But suppose he preached part of the time on the books of the Bible, part of the time on the great events of the Bible (some of them covering several chapters)? He could shift to the great men of the Bible (Abraham, Isaac, Jacob, Joseph, Moses, Joshua, Samuel, Saul, David, Solomon, Elijah, Isaiah, Jeremiah, Ezekiel, Daniel, Jesus, Peter, Paul, John), and then bring in the great chapters of the Bible. He could preach part of the time on paragraphs and texts and still cover the whole Bible in five to ten years. If he stayed longer, he could go back over the same ground in smaller portions. A plan like this would cause a pastor to stay longer, do better work, and get a call to a better field when it was God's time for him to move. Men like Matthew Henry, Joseph Parker, Alexander Maclaren, W. B. Riley, and William G. Coltman, did not move around much. They were too busy preaching through the Bible where they were.

A pastor trying to preach through the whole Bible does not worry too much about what to preach. He always has plenty of material before him. His problem will be to stay long enough and live long enough to preach it all. He can easily plan his preaching schedule, except for occasional break-ins, for several years to come.

Bernard Ramm expresses it like this: "Expository preaching makes sermon preparation easy. There is no frantic

8

search for a topic. There is a definite passage of Scripture to be handled, and a definite procedure for the handling. This does not mean that the preacher relentlessly follows his schedule. No, a crisis in the community, a special Sunday (Christmas, Easter), a special church need might call for a topical or textual sermon. But as a basis of his ministry, the expository preacher has a well-defined method which he systematically carries out and which for the most part relieves him of the anguish of knowing or deciding what to preach on next."[12]

If a preacher is to do lasting work, work that abides for eternity, expository preaching is his method. The Word of God is eternal and is settled forever in heaven. If the pastor can lash his people to the Scriptures in comprehensive and detailed knowledge, they can weather the storms of life and be useful Christians wherever they live. If the preacher hopes to stir young men and women to see the heavenly vision, to answer God's call to vocational Christian service, and in the years to come to have them serve in pastorates and in the mission fields, let him give them a preseminary training in his expository preaching.

If people are to know the God and Father of our Lord Jesus Christ they must meet Him in the Scriptures. They can know Him only vaguely through nature, conscience, and history. The God of the Bible is the only God who can save, sanctify, and glorify. Most church members know the Bible only as they learn it from their pastors, and they know only that God they conceive in their minds. Preachers must enlarge their conceptions of God. What a God He is as He walks through the Scriptures—the God of creation, judgment, election, grace, redemption, history and glory! Let preachers give their hearers a full-orbed view of God as they unfold the Scriptures in expository preaching!

Adolph Saphir said it well: "Thus nothing is more

needed in our days, both for the church and the world, than a faithful and deep exposition of Scripture, of the whole Scripture, of Scripture in its organic unity and comprehensive fulness, in order that by grace, mind, conscience, and heart may be convinced that here are revealed unto us thoughts higher than our thoughts, divine realities and blessings, things which eye hath not seen nor ear heard, neither have entered into the heart of man. And thus, while they who believe not will acknowledge that God is in us of a truth, the children of God will be kept stedfast and faithful; they will be furnished unto every good work, and forgetting the things that are behind, will press toward the mark for the prize of the high calling of God in Christ Jesus."[13]

If nothing else in this chapter motivates you to undertake a ministry of expository preaching, perhaps some of the testimonies to the value of expository preaching, as given in our survey, will do it. The last item on our questionnaire read: "If you have any personal testimony in favor of expository preaching, please state it briefly." Here are some of the testimonies:

It enriches the life of the preacher, and strengthens the faith of the congregation. The preacher can deal with problems when they are not sore spots.

It pleases and glorifies God because it points directly to Him, the source of all our help and blessings.

It gives greater variety and usually is more satisfying.

It enables people to recall in their own devotions what was said about the passage.

Encourages Bible reading, Bible study, and the use of the Bible in the church services.

Carries a ring of authority. Sharp and uncomfortable truths are more readily accepted when given from the Bible instead of as the thoughts of the minister.

10

The Holy Spirit can minister His Word to the people better than the preacher's words.

Keeps my preaching Bible-centered and meets real needs in congregation.

Needed to prevent religious illiteracy.

Best way to keep fresh in your preaching.

It refreshes me most and leaves a longer impression on the audience.

Produces sound Christians, good church members, and helps you touch problems with a constructive solution that is Scriptural.

Has won souls and has established God's Word, not the Mass, in the hearts of the people by the Holy Spirit (missionary in Mexico).

Produces the greatest fruit evangelistically and ethically. People want to know what the Bible teaches.

Your ministry gains power as you go: expanded lives, Bible reading and praying result.

Forces deeper research; opens the Scriptures more significantly.

The most powerful preaching; Spirit of God can use it best; provides its own main illustrations.

The best way to prevent too much of the minister showing up in the sermon.

It is the great need of today; it is preaching with authority.

It gives organized knowledge of the Bible as a Book.

Keeps preachers from overuse of more familiar portions of Scripture or using popular portions too often.

Dependence on the Holy Spirit greater in my case.

Best way to keep from riding hobbies and to preach the whole counsel of God.

What more can we say? The motives for expository preaching are many and powerful.

II

Power Through

DIVERSIFICATION

THE FEAR PREVAILS IN some minds that a program of expository preaching would grow monotonous. This could be a danger with some congregations, especially if the expository presentation were not well done. However, we have examples of men who have maintained their popularity and increased their congregations through continued expository preaching.

Harold J. Ockenga testified: "By the time I began my ministry in Park Street in 1936, I was primarily an expository preacher. Hence, I began at Matthew 1:1 and in twenty-one years have preached through the entire New Testament at my Sunday morning and Friday evening meetings."[1]

D. Martyn Lloyd-Jones preached sixty expository sermons on the Sermon on the Mount. Wilbur M. Smith reported that this same man preached for two years on sixty successive messages from Ephesians, chapters 1 and 2, and was going on to cover the next two chapters with the same thoroughness.[2]

The late Donald Grey Barnhouse said that he preached on Romans at the Sunday morning services, without a break, for three and one half years at the Tenth Presbyterian Church, Philadelphia; and that the congregation grew from a hundred or more to a full house.[3]

Other men of the past have done it successfully. For example, George Dana Boardman delivered "before his congregation, the First Baptist Church of Philadelphia, Pa., on successive Wednesday evenings . . . 640 lectures, going through every word of the New Testament, and then began a similar series on the Old Testament."[4]

Today's average congregation would tire of such long extended expository series, particularly if the preaching revealed some of the faults commonly charged against expository preaching: lack of unity, dry as dust, too exegetical, too long, no relevancy to today's problems, and not enough illustrations. But these are deficiencies that apply to other types of preaching too.

Many pastors and people need to be educated to expository preaching. Paul S. Rees writes: "It seems to me that a service sometimes overlooked is that of making Holy Scripture not only more understandable but more lovable. The light we must have; if, in addition, we can have the lure, so much the better."[5] Yes, indeed, a congregation can be brought not only to appreciate but to love expository preaching if it is really preaching.

But a preacher need not follow the same pattern in all his expository work. Many diversifications are possible and in the use of them he adds power to his pulpit ministry.

Jeff D. Ray suggested five varieties of expository preaching:

First, exegetical exposition which uses shorter passages and majors in grammatical and lexical study.

Second, doctrinal exposition which assembles all the major Bible passages on a subject and ascertains the meaning of each. The preacher arranges his findings in orderly and logical relations. We would classify this as topical preaching, but in the measure that it expounds each passage in its contextual-grammatical-historical meaning, it partakes of the expository.

14

Third, historical exposition which expounds the great events of the Bible regardless of the amount of Scripture involved.

Fourth, biographical exposition which deals with the order of events in a person's career.

Fifth, character exposition which may deal with the same person as the biographical exposition but this approach emphasizes the moral qualities and inner character of the individual.[6]

Harry Jeffs has a chapter devoted to methods of exposition. He suggests nine, as follows:

1. The running commentary
2. Continuous exposition through a book of the Bible
3. Exposition of related passages in a series
4. The message of a Bible book, one sermon per book
5. The expositor as a painter pointing up the story-pictures of the Bible
6. The preacher as a dramatist with great use of imagination and dramatic qualities
7. The Bible portrait gallery, preaching on the characters of the Bible
8. Analogical exposition, "in which the preacher does not so much draw out the primary sense of the text, as allow the text to suggest some analogous sense in which the principle of the text is seen to be operative." This method comes close to the spiritualizing and allegorical handlings which are questionable.
9. Devotional exposition which emphasizes the mystical and other-worldly elements of Christianity.[7]

Andrew W. Blackwood gives excellent guidance for expository preaching in chapters dealing with biographical sermons, paragraph sermons, a sermon series through a book of the Bible, chapter sermons, and Bible book sermons.[8]

Harry C. Mark suggests and illustrates many possibilities for topical, textual, and expository sermons. Within the expository mode, he suggests sermons of the telescopic period or age, book, chapter, section, historical, and word variety.[9]

Perry and Whitesell give five variations within the expository method, based upon the length of the passage discussed: single verses, paragraphs, chapters, thematic sections, and whole Bible books.[10]

Charles E. Faw's *A Guide to Biblical Preaching*[11] is an able discussion of preaching in a single sermon on the whole Bible, or one of its major divisions, or a Bible book, a part of a book, a paragraph, a sentence or a Biblical atom.

Since the Bible ranges over a vast area of subject matter, the expository preacher need not devote too long to any one type. If he wishes to skip around in the Bible, he can vary his individual sermons from an historical base to a legal one, from legal to dramatic, from dramatic to devotional, from devotional to wisdom, from wisdom to apocalyptic, from apocalyptic to poetic, from poetic to epistolary.

If the preacher enjoys preaching sermon series, he might have a series on the Ten Commandments, followed by one on the seven churches of Asia Minor, then on conversions in the Book of Acts. The number of varied sermon series possible is limited only by the resourcefulness of the preacher.

The expositor can further diversify his preaching by selecting different aims for his individual sermons. His pastoral calling, counseling, and meditation will reveal to him the needs of his congregation. As he preaches to these

16

needs he may take such general aims as the evangelistic, the doctrinal, the devotional, the inspirational, the corrective, or the consolatory. But within each of these general aims, he may wish to adopt more narrow and specific aims. Under the evangelistic aim, he may wish to unveil the nature of sin in one sermon, and to indicate the way of salvation in another. If the sermon is doctrinal, he may wish to preach from an expository passage on the work of the Holy Spirit in one sermon, and on obedience to the leading of the Spirit in another. The aim of the sermon will determine what Scripture passage to use and how to handle it. On the other hand, after the preacher has selected and studied a Bible passage, he may adopt a sermonic aim in line with what appears to him to be the aim of the passage. "All scripture is inspired by God and profitable for teaching, for reproof, for correction, and for training in righteousness, that the man of God may be complete, equipped for every good work" (II Timothy 3:16, RSV).

As we study the sermons of great expository preachers we learn that each one developed his own methods and techniques. No two are exactly alike. All of them have purposed to unfold, illuminate, and apply the Scriptures, but they go about it in a variety of ways. Not all their procedures can be commended, but if we can discover their distinguishing techniques, emphases, or approaches, we can decide whether or not we wish to adopt anything from them. Other homileticians may not agree with all of our findings at this point, but we hope our review will prove thought-provoking; and that students of expository preaching will learn some helpful methods.

The disciplined approach—Alexander Maclaren. We use this term because he so thoroughly dedicated himself to an expository ministry, and so doggedly disciplined himself in it. Each day throughout his life he read one Bible chapter in Hebrew and another in Greek. He shut himself in his study every day of the week and devoted many exacting hours to the preparation of each sermon. He did very little pastoral calling and administrative work, nor did he travel around the world preaching in other places. He believed that if people wanted to hear him, they would come to Union Chapel in Manchester, England, where he was pastor for forty-five years, and occasional preacher for six more years.

Maclaren's *Expositions of Holy Scripture* attains the highest level of expository excellence and homiletical finish. E. C. Dargan wrote of him: "No critical or descriptive account can do justice to the excellence and power of Maclaren's preaching . . . . In contents and form these sermons are models of modern preaching. The exegesis of Scripture . . . is thorough and accurate. The analysis, while not obtrusive, is always complete, satisfying, clear. . . . Maclaren's style has all the rhetorical qualities of force, clearness, and beauty . . . Maclaren's sermons . . . are so complete as expositions of the Bible, so lofty in tone, so free from that which is merely temporary and catchy, both in thought and style, that they can not but appeal to the minds of men long after the living voice has ceased to impress them upon living hearts."[12]

He has been called the prince of expositors and the king of preachers. W. Robertson Nicoll, editor of *The Expositor's Bible* and *The Expositor's Greek Testament,* wrote: "It is difficult to believe that Dr. Maclaren's *Expositions* will ever be superseded. Will there ever again be such a combination of spiritual insight, of scholarship, of passion, of style, of keen intellectual power?"[13]

Maclaren's exegesis is always sound and thorough, his outlines clear but seldom striking, his illustrations few and short, his applications strong but rather impersonal. His best expository work is claimed to be that on Colossians in *The Expositor's Bible*. There he devotes twenty-six sermons to Colossians, but in his *Expositions of Holy Scripture,* covering the whole Bible, there are only nine sermons on this same epistle, five of them on the first chapter.

Andrew W. Blackwood believes that Maclaren's preaching was mostly textual until he passed middle life, and that the shift to regular expository work came in his fifty-seventh year.[14] Most of Maclaren's sermons in *Expositions of Holy Scripture* seem to be textual at first glance, but closer examination shows that he always uses his text in the light of the larger context and his handling is really expository.

The contextual principle—G. Campbell Morgan. He never handled any text, large or small, without closely relating it to its total context. By doing so he was often able to develop fresh and convincing interpretations of familiar passages. Many people considered Morgan the greatest of modern expository preachers. Wilbur M. Smith wrote: "For 40 years, beginning at the first decade of our century, the entire Christian world acknowledged that the greatest Biblical expositor known in the pulpits of both England and America was Dr. G. Campbell Morgan."[15]

Morgan's expository sermons are best represented in the ten volumes of *The Westminster Pulpit*. Here are nearly 300 of his expository sermons. Most of them are based on a single text of one, two or three verses of Scripture, but before Morgan has finished his sermon he has thoroughly explored his text grammatically, contextually, and theologically. They are expository sermons.

Don M. Wagner wrote a small book on Morgan's expository method. His conclusion is: "Dr. G. Campbell Morgan's expository method is the application of the context principle of Bible study. A definition of the context principle indicates that the hypothesis contains a great deal more than that which appears on the surface. Context principle is the interpretation of a given passage in the light of the text which surrounds it, diminishing in importance as one proceeds from the near to the far context. Two fundamental principles are involved in putting this context principle to work; they are analysis and synthesis. Analysis takes apart and classifies or describes each part; synthesis assembles the parts in a logical order."[16]

Before preaching from a book of the Bible, Morgan would read it through from forty to fifty times. He would survey, condense, expand and dissect it.

Morgan taught and preached the Bible from almost every angle. His books on Matthew, Mark, Luke, John, Acts, I and II Corinthians, Hosea and Jeremiah are not fully sermonic but are pure expositions. His *Great Chapters of the Bible* contains the substance of sermons on forty-nine chapters of the Bible. In his *Living Messages of the Books of the Bible* there is a sermonic study on every book of the Bible. *The Great Physician* sermonizes on the soul-winning and healing miracles of Jesus. *Searchlights From the Word* takes one text from each chapter of the Bible and explains the chapter around that verse.

In his little book on *Preaching* Morgan affirmed that truth, clarity and passion were the essentials of a sermon. He claimed that getting the outline was the most important part of the homiletical process. Like Maclaren, Morgan dedicated himself to lifelong Bible study. Who was the greater expositor, Maclaren or Morgan? Opinions differ. Both disciplined themselves to highest achievement in Biblical exposition.

The balanced approach—Frederick W. Robertson. Although Robertson died when he was thirty-seven years old,

A. W. Blackwood thinks of him "as the most influential preacher thus far in the English-speaking world."[17] In six years of expository work he covered only I and II Samuel, Acts, Genesis, and I and II Corinthians. He died practically unknown outside his parish at Brighton, England, but his stature has continued to increase through his printed sermons. His greatness is hard to explain. His sermons grip one with their plaintive sadness, rugged honesty, Scriptural discernment, forward movement, and utter simplicity. E. C. Dargan says of his sermonic method: "He made a careful expository study of the Scripture, usually taking full notes. The division is nearly always twofold. He was fond of thinking in pairs and antithesis."[18]

And James R. Blackwood wrote: "In choosing his text and in outlining the message, Robertson laid stress on the principle of balance. Partly for this reason he excelled in writing a sermon with only two main parts."[19]

And again, James R. Blackwood writes about the tested sermonizing formula of Robertson: "He took one clear thought and let it dominate the sermon; he developed it positively, not negatively; suggestively, not dogmatically; from the inward to the outward; and with frequent use of balance and contrast."[20]

E. C. Dargan would add this further word: "In spite of their condensed and imperfect form, the sermons (as printed) have great literary charm. The style is pure, glowing, clear, attractive. The homiletical excellence of these sermons is beyond dispute. Careful interpretation of Scripture, simple twofold division, and clearly marked subdivisions, give a unity of structure and a completeness of treatment notwithstanding the condensed form."[21]

One of Robertson's expository talents, according to F. R. Webber, was this: "Where many preachers begin with a doctrine, and then search for proof-texts, Robertson began

21

with a text, probed for its meaning, and drew doctrine out of it."[22]

Robertson has a famous sermon on "The Loneliness of Christ," based on John 16:31-32. He divides it into two main points: we meditate on the loneliness of Christ; on the temper of His solitude.

The imaginative approach—Joseph Parker. Author of many volumes of sermons, he is known especially for his *Parker's People's Bible*, twenty-seven volumes covering most of the Bible. He was unique, eccentric, individualistic but popular, eloquent, energetic, oratorical, imaginative, versatile, intense in feelings and strongly evangelical. He said: "Of all the kinds of preaching, I love expository the most. You will understand this from the fact that during the last seven years I have expounded most of the first two books of the Pentateuch, the whole book of Nehemiah, the whole of Ecclesiastes, and nearly half of the Gospel of Matthew."[23]

Parker's sermons resemble the running commentary, Biblical homilies with fair evidence of an outline. He does not go into close exegesis and careful interpretation, but his material is rich, original, colorful, vivid, and exciting. His let his imagination soar but kept it under the control of reality.

Alexander Gammie wrote of Parker: "And there was always the element of the unexpected in what he said and how he said it. Yet there was something more, very much more, than all that. He was a supreme interpreter of the Scriptures. His *People's Bible* is a mine for preachers, because of its freshness and originality and insight. Often by a flash of intuition, inspiration, or genius—call it what you will—he made texts sparkle with a new meaning."[24]

Though not classified as expository preachers, Alexander Whyte and T. DeWitt Talmage both are highly imagina-

22

tive. This quality is developed further in our chapter on imagination.

The pivot text method—F. B. Meyer. Meyer was a popular, devotional-type, expository preacher. When he was still a young man, his friend, Charles Birrell, said to him: "I advise you to do as I have done for the last 30 years— become an expositor of Scripture. You will always retain your freshness and will build a strong and healthy church."[25]

He took the advice and majored in expository preaching. Meyer specialized in expository preaching on Bible personalities, and his published volumes included the lives of Abraham, Jacob, Joseph, Moses, Joshua, David, Samuel, Elijah, Jeremiah, John the Baptist, Paul and Peter. His method of preparing to preach through a book of the Bible was to study that book intensely for two or three months, reading it repeatedly until its central lesson became clear to him. Next he divided the book into sections and subsections, each containing a well-developed thought. Then he sought out the pivot text in each section, a verse which was terse, crisp, bright and short, one that could be easily remembered and quoted. He developed his exposition around that pivot text relating to it all the main elements of the surrounding text.

Meyer gave a certain graphic or pictorial quality to Scripture interpretation, put glowing color into it, and invested truth with the radiant freshness of new truth. Having heard him preach, Alexander Gammie had this impression: "Quietly, persuasively, serenely, and in silver tones he proclaimed his message. The phrasing was simple, with the simplicity of the art which conceals art, the imagery peaceful and pastoral 'like an English valley washed with sunlight.' . . . Everything was intimate, tender and appealing."[26]

Robert G. Lee wrote of Meyer's books: ". . . his books have been a source of stimulation for my mind, of comfort for my heart, of encouragement in times when the roads were rough, the hills high, the valleys deep and dark. I believe every preacher who does not have and does not read the books of Dr. Meyer cheats himself, impoverishes his spiritual life, and makes less valiant his faith. . . . I urge you to purchase, to read, to search, to study all of Dr. Meyer's books. If you obey my insistent urging, you will thank me."[27]

The inverted pyramid method—Donald Grey Barnhouse. He affirmed: "I believe that the only way to understand any given passage in the Word of God is to take the whole Bible and place the point of it, like an inverted pyramid, on that passage, so that the weight of the entire Word rests upon a single verse, or indeed a single word."[28]

Barnhouse went into great detail. His expository series on Romans took three and one half years of Sunday morning preaching. He says that his method of preparation was to read thirty or forty leading commentaries on Romans; use some twenty translations in English, French, and German; plus grammatical research in *Strong's Concordance*, *Thayer's Greek Lexicon*, and the *Englishman's Greek Concordance*. He sometimes has two sermons on the same text. On Romans 5:2 he has six, and on 5:5 he has seven. On Romans, chapter 1, he has twenty-seven sermons, and on Romans, chapter 5, twenty-seven. Inevitably some of these sermons seem to be more topical than expository, but the expository aspect is in the careful, detailed, and painstaking verse-by-verse unfolding and application of the book of Romans in the light of the rest of the Bible.

The author-centered approach—Paul S. Rees. In his expository series on Philippians, entitled *The Adequate Man,* he believes that this epistle is a remarkable self-portrait

24

of its author, so he expounds the epistle in five sermons setting forth differing characteristics of the Apostle Paul: "The Art of the Heart," "The Affectionate Man," "The Alert Man," "The Aspiring Man," and "The Adequate Man."[29] This author-centered approach can be used with many parts of the Bible. Men like F. B. Meyer, William M. Taylor and Clovis G. Chappell have followed it in their biographical-expository volumes.

The single-subject expository handling—Roy L. Laurin. This method was used by Laurin in a number of his expositions of New Testament books. He selected the idea of "Life" as being a wedge to open these books. He expounds Romans under the theme, *Where Life Begins,* II Corinthians under *Where Life Endures,* I Corinthians under *Where Life Matures,* Philippians under *Where Life Advances,* Colossians under *Where Life Is Established,* and I John under *Life At Its Best.* On the whole, his sermons are true to expository ideals and well worth reading.

As an example, in his book on II Corinthians, *Where Life Endures,*[30] he includes thirteen sermons covering the epistle. The first seven are under the general title, "The Endurance of the Christian," and the specific subtitles are: "The Life That Endures Adversity," "The Life That Endures Discipline," "The Life That Endures Experience," "The Life That Endures Service," "The Life That Endures Dying," "The Life That Endures Living," and "The Life That Endures Chastening." The danger of this method, in less able hands, might be to force the Scriptures into artificial molds.

The backgrounds emphasis—George Adam Smith and *Harris E. Kirk.* An Old Testament scholar from Scotland, Smith was rather liberal in his view of the Scriptures, but he was widely recognized as a great expositor. He contributed the volumes on Isaiah and on the minor prophets to *The Expositor's Bible.* As author of the famous *Histor-*

ical Geography of the Holy Land, Smith put great emphasis upon the historical and geographical situation in back of any Scripture passage. Even though his work is somewhat outdated by recent research, one has to admit that he makes the Scriptures come alive as he puts them into their proper setting.

Edgar DeWitt Jones wrote of him: "As a preacher Dr. Smith was Biblical, expository, and exegetical. There was clarity and simplicity in his discourses, the illustrative material was choice, and he was equally at home in a rural church or on a university occasion."[31]

He gave the Lyman Beecher Lectures on preaching at Yale in 1899 under the title, "Modern Criticism and the Preaching of the Old Testament."

Harris E. Kirk, for over forty years pastor of the Franklin Street Presbyterian Church, Baltimore, also went in heavily for proper background material. As the author listened to him in July, 1946, at the Princeton Summer Conference for Ministers, he was deeply impressed by Kirk's extensive knowledge and use of background material. He told us: "Get into the great trends and movements of Biblical history, the great tidal forces and rhythms. Learn to float on the fluid element of God's grace in history and providence. Get the relationship of the Bible to the land itself, and the relationship of the land to ancient civilizations."

The running commentary method has many users. One of the best known of modern times was Harry A. Ironside. He published sermonic commentaries on nearly all of the Bible. As pastor of the Moody Church, Chicago, for eighteen and one half years, he was one of the most popular Bible-teaching preachers in America. Usually he went from verse to verse, or from section to section of a passage, and he regularly preached straight through books of the Bible.

26

What he lacked in structural strength he made up for in powerful explanation, illustration, application, and exhortation. His sermons are racy reading, full of spiritual truth and interesting illustrations.

William R. Newell, who gave us expositions of Romans, Hebrews, and Revelation, was a running commentary preacher who sought to dig deeply into the Word by verse-to-verse comments.

John Chrysostom, called "the golden-mouthed," was a great expository preacher who covered most of the Bible in running commentary sermons, as did Martin Luther.

John Calvin and Ulrich Zwingli, the Protestant reformers, used the running commentary method to cover the books of the Bible. Regardless of the defects of this method in structure and unity, it has a noble history. If a preacher gives it thorough preparation and powerful presentation, it will still have popular appeal. But we think there is a better way available, and we shall set it forth fully in the chapters to follow.

The lessons method—William M. Taylor and J. C. Ryle. Taylor twice gave the Lyman Beecher Lectures on preaching at Yale: first in 1876, on "The Ministry of the Word," and again in 1886, on "The Scottish Pulpit." He published popular and useful volumes on *The Miracles of Our Saviour* and *The Parables of Our Saviour,* as well as several on Bible characters. His expository method was to present a thorough discussion of his Scripture passage in explanation and interpretation, then point out the practical lessons and drive them home.

In his sermon on "The Healing of the Gadarene Demoniac," he gives twelve pages of exposition and uses four and one half pages to set forth four lessons and apply them.

J. C. Ryle was bishop of Liverpool. His four-volume set, *Expository Thoughts on the Gospels,* takes the reader through the four gospels. Ryle takes a passage of several verses and plunges into a discussion of it, drawing from it three, four, or five practical applications. His treatments are shorter than sermons, running only about four pages each, but at the end of each he appends two or three pages of explanatory notes. His points are sometimes more suggestive and inferential than those directly taught by the passage, but they always strike one with force and appeal. Ryle majors on application rather than explanation, argument, or illustration. His method is popular and helpful but it has to be used with restraint.

The analytical method—W. H. Griffith Thomas. He was a Bible-teaching preacher par excellence, strong on structural outlines. He believed that Alexander Maclaren's expositions were the finest models of all expository preaching. Thomas insisted that three features were needed in any expository presentation: (1) it should concern only the salient features; (2) mainly it should concern the spiritual meaning; (3) it should always have a searching message.[32] Thomas' commentaries on Genesis, Romans, Acts, and Colossians, and his books on the lives and writings of Peter and John will furnish abundant outlines and much fine commentary material for the expository preacher or Sunday school teacher.

W. Graham Scroggie is also an outstanding analyst of the Bible. His works on various parts of the Bible are less sermonic than analytical.

The exegetical method—A. T. Robertson and William Barclay. Robertson was the outstanding Greek scholar of America in his day. He could go into the Greek words of the New Testament and expound them with practical applications more easily than the average preacher can do it in English. His homely but pointed comments held the attention of crowds. He has left us exegetical-sermonic commentaries on Mark's Gospel, James, Philippians, and Colossians. He also wrote on the lives of John the Baptist, Mark, Paul, Peter and John, as well as other more technical New Testament studies. His set on *Word Pictures in the New Testament* should be used by every expository preacher. In 1934 he published a volume of sermons entitled *Passing On the Torch and Other Sermons*. Many of these have good outlines and are more homiletical than most of his other works. Robertson's writings are rich source material for expository preachers.

William Barclay of Scotland has produced a splendid series of small commentaries on the different parts and books of the New Testament. They are written in a popular and interesting style, and are exegetical and semi-sermonic. It is not hard to believe that Barclay used most of this material in expository preaching. Every expository preacher should obtain the Barclay commentaries and use them.

The exegetical method involves the danger of becoming too technical and too dry for popular use, but in the hands of Robertson or Barclay it does not.

The stylistic emphasis—John Henry Jowett. One of the world's most renowned preachers, he possessed all the features of homiletical perfection, but he put major emphasis on style. His hobby was the study of words and he would write, rewrite, correct, and rewrite in order to perfect his style. Most of his sermons seem to be textual but when one studies them, one finds the exegesis so careful, the contextual relations so recognized, and the rhetorical elements so balanced, that the sermons fit the expository category. Jowett published a large number of books and hundreds of sermons in Christian periodicals and magazines. His expository genius is best illustrated in *The High Calling*, an exposition of Philippians; *The Epistles of*

St. Peter; and *The Whole Armor of God,* expounding a part of Ephesians 6.

The evangelistic method—William B. Riley and *George W. Truett.* Both men were Baptist pastors in their respective pulpits for nearly fifty years, and both were intensely evangelistic. They turned the Scriptures to evangelistic ends.

Riley was more truly an expository preacher. He was the author of many books and pamphlets but his supreme contribution to expository preaching is his forty-volume set, *The Bible of the Expositor and Evangelist.* The whole Bible has been covered in this set, though not every passage by any means. The sermons are well outlined and ably illustrated. Most of them throb with evangelistic passion and appeal.

Truett was a greater pulpiteer than Riley. In fact, many considered him the greatest preacher in America in his time. His soul and sermons fairly flamed with evangelistic power. If one heard him preach at the zenith of his power, one could never forget it. Many of his sermons have been printed or reprinted in recent years. They are usually textual but he always paid careful attention to his text, and sometimes he became expository.

Charles H. Spurgeon belongs in the evangelistic category too. Most of his sermons were textual, but now and then he became expository, and in every case he used his text for more than a starting point.

With these suggestions for diversification, we believe that any expositor should be able to stay out of the rut of monotony and be able to use the power of variety yet still remain expository.

III

Power Through
EXPLANATION

ONE OF THE FUNDAMENTAL purposes of expository preaching is explanation, or exposition of the Word of God. The expository preacher seeks to find the true and exact meaning of the Scriptures and to set that meaning against life today.

The Bible is mostly a foreign book to us. Coming out of the dim and misty past it tells about strange lands, peoples, customs, events and ideas. We need to explain many of its words, phrases, sentences, names, places, movements, persons, ideas, and situations. Every area of the Biblical world will need explanation: historical, geographical, sociological, theological, biographical, cultural, literary, cosmological, psychological, archaeological, and grammatical. But rarely will we need to use all of these forms in a single sermon.

Many expository sermons will include a large amount of explanation, and others very little. The preacher should learn to compress the explanation and not waste time in it. Sometimes he may need to weigh different explanations against each other, but usually he will do better to arrive at the best explanation he possibly can and then present it. Odd or extreme explanations should nearly always be avoided. The popular mind has an instinct for sensing sound explanations and appreciating them. The average hearer will esteem no part of the sermon more than good explanation. People revere the Bible and wish to increase their understanding of it.

To gain a full and complete understanding of a passage from the Bible in order to explain it clearly and forcefully, five areas of investigation may be involved.

I. Background Data

This is information about the passage. Several important items comprise the background materials.

1. The writer: Who wrote this passage? What type of person was he? His importance? Any writing characteristics or emphases?
2. The speaker: Is he different from the writer?
3. The addressees: To whom written? To whom spoken? What significance?
4. The time: What year, month, day, hour, if known?
5. The place: Where did this occur, or where spoken or written? Any significance to this place? Any archaeological light?
6. The occasion: What caused this passage to be written?
7. The aim: What was the purpose of the speaker or writer, or both?
8. The literary form: Is the passage prose or poetry? Is it parable or history? Is it legislation or exhortation? Is it apocalytic or drama?
9. The historical setting: Amidst what historical milieu is this passage set? What bearing does this have on the interpretation of the passage?
10. The revelational stage: How much revelation of God had been given at this point? Was it under law or under grace? Was it before Pentecost or after?

Many of these data can be found in the passage itself or

in the nearby context. Others must be gleaned from Bible dictionaries, encyclopedias, histories, commentaries, and geographies. H. H. Halley's *Bible Handbook* is a compact and reliable source for many of these items.

Let us apply this procedure to Luke 18:1-8: the parable of the unjust judge and the widow who cried to him for justice.

1. The writer: He was Luke, the physician and companion of Paul; a Gentile; a cultured and reliable historian.
2. The speaker: Jesus.
3. The addressees: The disciples of Jesus (17:22, 37). The Gospel of Luke was addressed to Theophilus (1:3), but probably intended for Gentile readers.
4. The time: During the later Perean ministry of Jesus, about 29 A.D., not long before Jesus' crucifixion.
5. The place: On the way to Jerusalem while He was going through Samaria or Galilee (17:11).
6. The occasion: He had been talking to the Pharisees about when the Kingdom of God would come, and then to His disciples (17:20-22). Luke alone records this parable of the widow and the judge.
7. The aim: The aim seems to be to urge His disciples to faithfulness in prayer while they await His second coming.
8. The literary form: A parable, or a story, which may not actually have occurred, but it was true to life and often such events did occur.
9. The historical setting: The Roman Empire ruled the world. The Jews were subject to it, and hated it. Perhaps the fall of Jerusalem and its destruction in 70 A.D. had not yet taken place, though some believe it had occurred. Before the crucifixion and before Pentecost.

33

10. The revelational stage: This passage has an apocalyptic setting. He had been talking about His second coming in chapter 17 and refers to it again in this passage. These disciples were under the law. Christ was nearing the end of His earthly ministry.

II. Exegetical Data

This concerns information in the passage. What is the true text? the right translation? the proper interpretation?

The easiest place to begin is with the various English translations of the Bible. Read the passage first in the King James Version, then in the American Standard, the Revised Standard, the New English Bible, the American Translation (University of Chicago Press), the James Moffatt translation, the Berkeley Version, and in the Amplified New Testament or Old Testament. For the New Testament many other modern translations exist: Charles B. Williams, Helen B. Montgomery, R. F. Weymouth, J. B. Phillips, the Twentieth Century, etc. If the pastor can read German, French, Spanish, Swedish, or any other foreign language, he should read his passage in these tongues.

If he knows Hebrew and Greek, he should go into the original text. Here he will use his lexicons, grammars and concordances. *The Englishman's Greek Concordance* or *The Englishman's Hebrew and Chaldee Concordance* will give him every occurrence of any word in Greek or Hebrew. J. H. Thayer's *Greek-English Lexicon of the New Testament* is a standard help, but has been somewhat superseded by the newer W. F. Arndt and F. W. Gingrich *A Greek-English Lexicon of the New Testament and Other Early Christian Literature*. Either Robert Young's *Anallytical Concordance to the Bible* or James Strong's *Exhaustive Concordance of the Bible* will help to understand the original languages even though one has never studied them.

The next step should take the student to the exegetical word studies and commentaries by A. T. Robertson, Marvin R. Vincent, W. E. Vine, or Kenneth S. Wuest. The preacher should keep notes on his exegetical studies, and add to them other ideas for illustrations, explanation, argument, or application that occur to him.

Let us look at Luke 18:1-8 and indicate some of the exegetical data concerning it.

v.1: It is a parable, or story, of Jesus, not to be pressed too far in all details. Does "ought always to pray" mean to pray all the time without ceasing, or does it mean to pray at all times, or on all occasions? The Greek word *pantote,* for "always," occurs forty-two times in the New Testament. The King James Version translates it as "always" most of the times, but sometimes as "ever" and "evermore." Thayer gives the meaning as "at all times, always, ever"; James H. Moulton's and George Milligan's *The Vocabulary of the Greek New Testament* gives "at all times, always" as the meaning, while Arndt and Gingrich say, "always, at all times." Paul uses this word ten times for either giving thanks or praying for people. William Taylor seems to be right that it means to pray on all occasions and under all circumstances, not all the time without stopping to do anything else. ". . . and not to faint" means "not to give in to evil, to turn coward and lose heart," observed A. T. Robertson.

v.2: ". . . a judge who neither feared God nor regarded man" (RSV), "who had no reverence for God nor respect for men" (WILLIAMS). William Barclay says that he was not a Jewish judge, but: "This judge was one of these paid magistrates appointed either by Herod or by the Romans. Such judges were notorious. Unless a plaintiff had influence and money to bribe his way to a verdict, he had no hope of ever getting his case settled."[1]

v.3: ". . . a widow in that city who kept coming to him and saying, 'vindicate me against my adversary' " (RSV). Jesus does not say who the widow was, but Alexander Whyte, in his highly imaginative way, says this: "There were many widows who had adversaries in our Lord's land and day, and He must have known more than one of them. His own mother Mary may very well have been one of them. Who knows but that she herself was this very widow with an adversary? Nothing is more likely."[2]

"Avenge me of mine adversary" (KJV) means "Give me justice and protection from my opponent" (WILLIAMS).

The Interpreter's Bible comments: "The woman had no money to bribe the unscrupulous judge, and no power to bully him, but she had persistence: she badgered him. Day by day he 'took a beating' from her."[3]

v.4: The wicked judge held out against her pleadings as long as he could, admitting that he cared not for God or man.

v.5: "Yet because this widow troubleth me" (KJV); "bothers me" (RSV); "yet this woman is such a nuisance (PHILLIPS). ". . . lest by her continual coming she weary me" (KJV); "she will wear me out" (RSV); "her continual visits will be the death of me!" (PHILLIPS). The Greek word *hupopiadza* here means "to hit under the eye" or "to give a black eye." R. C. H. Lenski states metaphorically, "lest finally by coming she be knocking me out," not literally, but by her everlasting coming she will break down the judge's resistance and move him to act.

The Abingdon Bible Commentary says: "The magistrate is not seriously afraid of assault and battery in open court, but was afraid of a scene, by which his dignity would be so badly compromised that, whenever he sat there, people would remember how he was bearded by a widow!"[4]

v.6-7: Jesus called attention to the unrighteous judge in order to contrast his character and conduct sharply with the righteous character and merciful conduct of God.

v.7: God will give justice to His elect who persist in praying. He will not delay long but will vindicate them speedily as He counts time. Barclay says that this does not mean that God always answers immediately. A father must refuse the requests of his children at times, knowing that they do not ask aright. God knows the future perfectly and with it knows exactly when to give what is good for us.

v.8: "... will he find faith on earth?" (RSV), or "the faith" (Greek). When Christ comes, will He find His disciples holding out in prayer for His vindication? Will their faith stand this test? The whole passage is apocalyptic.

Norval Geldenhuys comments: "He now teaches in this parable that when His coming is apparently slow in taking place, believers are not to become discouraged, but should persist in prayer, knowing that He will indeed come at the right time and will answer their supplication. . . ."[5]

R. C. H. Lenski says that the elect are always precious to God, but He does not always act to vindicate them with the speed they wish. With God a thousand years is as one day and one day as a thousand years (II Peter 3:8-9). God may wish in this time to discipline His elect until they are mature and patient, but at the end, when Christ returns, He will act with speed and justice. Lenski holds that Jesus did not mean to teach that "the faith" would not exist when

37

He returns. He only raises the question concerning it in order to stimulate His children to keep on crying for justice until He appears.

III. Structural Data

The preacher should determine the thought structure of his passage. What is its subject? What are its possible themes? The subject is broad and general, but the theme is a partitioning of the subject. What are the major ideas in the passage and how are they related to each other? What minor ideas support each major idea? He should outline the passage, giving the major ideas Roman numbers and the minor ones Arabic numbers. This will reveal to him the structure or analysis of his passage.

The result of this procedure is only a skeleton, not a sermon outline. He has arranged the ideas in the order in which they occur in the passage. This structural analysis may be a long step toward a sermon outline but it still lacks the unity, balance, progress and impact of an outline. He has before him in skeletal form the ideas which he will probably use in making his sermon outline; and in the background and exegetical data he has much of the material he will need to develop his outline.

When we look at Luke 18:1-8, we ask, What is it about? The answer is, prayer. What kind of prayer? Persistent praying. Our subject then is prayer, and the theme, persistent praying. Since Luke calls it a parable, we have the heading for our structural outline.

A Parable of Persistent Praying

The thesis is plainly stated in verse 1, ". . . men ought always to pray, and not to faint" (KJV).

    I. The judge, v.2
        1. Lived in a city, v.2

    2. Did not fear God, v.2

    3. Did not regard man, v.2

  II.   The widow, v.3

    1. Lived in the same city, v.3

    2. Came to the judge, kept coming, v.3

  III.   The widow's prayer, v.3

    1. She had a definite request, v.3

    2. She kept coming with it, vv.3,5

    3. She asked to be avenged, or to have justice from her opponent in a lawsuit, v.3

  IV.   The judge's reaction, vv.4-5

    1. Having no fear of God and no respect for man, he refused to pay any attention, v.4

    2. The widow kept bothering him with her case, vv.3,5

    3. Not wishing to be pestered to death, he yielded and gave her justice, v.5

  V.   Jesus' lesson, vv.6-8

    1. Hear what the unjust judge said and did, v.6

    2. Let this be reason to know that God, the righteous Judge, will do the very opposite, v.7

    3. He will give justice to His elect, v.7

    4. God is patient with them and will avenge them speedily, v.8

  CONCLUSION: Let the elect maintain the faith that cries to God day and night and He will give them justice at the return of Christ.

IV. Contextual Data

What is the relation of the Scripture passage under discussion to its surrounding material? Unless a Bible passage consists of a series of disjointed proverbs or exhortations, its ideas are interconnected over a long stretch. The whole context should be studied in order to understand the meaning of any part, with the immediate context the most important. As the context becomes farther removed from the passage, it is likely to have less bearing on it. But certain characteristic ideas, phrases, and words may run through a whole book of the Bible, including the text the preacher is considering. The words *life, light, love,* and *believe* recur with great frequency in John's writings. We have seen that one great factor in G. Campbell Morgan's expository power was his loyalty to the contextual principle.

Looking at Luke 18:1-8 again, we see that its context is quite important. It immediately follows Jesus' discussion of the coming Kingdom and the end of the age in Luke 17:20-37. Jesus' interpretation of the parable links up with the apocalyptic idea (18:8). The parable of the Pharisee and the publican praying in the temple immediately follows our Scripture passage (18:9-14). Jesus seems to be teaching that true prayer is not only necessary in the light of His coming, but that it should be persistent and sincere.

Our text is set in Luke's Gospel which is the gospel of prayer and praise, the gospel of the poor, the outcasts and the widows. Luke was especially hard on the rich and sympathetic to the poor. The judge was no doubt rich and the widow quite poor. God will hear the praying poor.

V. Cross Reference Data

Now that the expositor has the data *about* the passage, *within* the passage, and *around* the passage, we suggest that he compare it with other similar references in the Bible. This will enrich his understanding, give him fresh insight, and furnish Biblical support.

While this parable occurs nowhere else in the Bible, we do have a similar story in Luke 11:5-13. There a man asks bread of a friend in order to take care of a guest. The friend does not wish to get up in the middle of the night

40

to help him, but because of his importunity the friend does. A friend can be moved to help by importunate asking. In our parable, an enemy can be moved by persistence. George A. Buttrick treats these two stories together in the same sermon, entitled, "The God Who Answers Prayer."[6]

When we look up some of the Greek words in this parable in *The Englishman's Greek Concordance,* we find that the word "to pray" in 18:1 is used some eighty times in the New Testament. The word "to faint" occurs also in II Corinthians 4:1, 4:16, Galatians 6:9, Ephesians 3:13, and II Thessalonians 3:13; showing wherein Christians may faint, or cave in. In 18:2 the word for "judge" is used often of men, but sometimes of God, as in Acts 10:42, II Timothy 4:8, Hebrews 12:23, and James 5:9. In 18:3 the word for "avenge" or "vindicate" is used four other times, showing the stress put on it. The word for "cry" is used in 18:7, in 18:38 and other places in the New Testament to mean "to cry aloud." The word for "bear long" (KJV), or "delay long over them" (RSV)—*makrothumeo* (Greek)—occurs eight other times in the New Testament in the verb form and fourteen other places in the noun form, and usually means "patience" or "longsuffering."

The writer does not insist that all these steps must necessarily be followed, or that this is the only way to compile the essential data for explaining a passage of Scripture, but this method will do it without overlooking anything, and will give the expositor assurance that he has done justice to his passage. The expositor might combine all these steps into one but it is doubtful that he would save any time or do it any better. However one does it, the main thing is to gather all this information and evaluate it thoroughly before attempting to speak on a text of Scripture.

When a preacher is preaching serially through a book of the Bible, he will need very little additional background data as he goes from passage to passage, for he has already considered most of that in his opening sermon. But the exegetical, structural, contextual, and cross reference material must be gathered for each passage he expounds.

We will not deal with hermeneutics, the science of sound Biblical interpretation, any more than to affirm that the expositor should be familiar with right principles of handling his explanatory data. He should have utmost confidence in the Bible, handle it reverently, and interpret it with spiritual insight. He will pay attention to the unfolding progressive revelation of the Bible, its essential unity, its various types of literature, and the centrality of Christ in the Scriptures. He will be wary about imposing rigid theological systems upon the Bible or of following those who do. He will seek the basic historical-contextual-grammatical interpretation of every passage in the light of the total teaching of the Scriptures.

The expositor will make notes on how others have explained different parts of this passage (Luke 18:1-8). William Taylor wrote: "The church on earth must never allow herself to become so hopeless and unbelieving, in regard to the second coming of her Lord, as to give up praying for that great consummation, when all her wrongs shall be redressed, and all her troubles shall be brought to a blessed and everlasting end. That is the great lesson of the parable, and it is to that the Saviour reverts when, as he concludes, he says, 'Nevertheless, when the Son of man cometh shall he find *that* faith?' for in the original, the article is used, and the reference is to such faith as will continue to the end looking and praying for the coming of the Son of man 'upon the earth.'"[7]

G. Campbell Morgan says:

We must not forget the connection of the parable with teaching He had recently given. He had been speaking of the fact that in the day of His final Manifestation things would be going on in the world just as they had been in the days of Noah, and in the days of Lot. Consequently, the age in which these men were called upon to live would be days of great difficulty. The parable, then, is a revelation of what is necessary for the life of faith, in an age which is not conducive to faith. In such an age, prayer is the very essence of life. Under such circumstances, our Lord says, in effect, there is one alternative offered to us, prayer or fainting. Our Lord's outlook upon the age, and of the life of His people through that age, is that unless men pray, they will faint.

It may be asked, How can people always pray? The answer is that we must understand what prayer is. Prayer is far more than uttering words. I can pray when I do not think I am praying. We can pray without any words at all. Prayer, in the last analysis, is the urge of the life towards God, and spiritual things. . . . Prayer literally means to wish forward. Prayer, then, is desiring towards the ultimate, the urge that for ever masters life for the coming of the Kingdom of God, and the victory of all things spiritual. Now, said Jesus, Unless your life is of that nature, you will faint.[8]

J. C. Ryle writes this illuminating sentence: "It is prayer without fainting, during the long weary interval between the first and second advents, which Jesus is urging His disciples to keep up."[9]

Alexander Whyte mingles strong imagination with explanation when he writes: "It was her orphaned and starving children that made their mother to be like a she-bear robbed of her whelps. Avenge me of mine adversary! She stood in the way of the unjust judge's chariot all day and cried out, Avenge me of mine adversary! She burst in upon the business of his court and cried, Avenge me of mine adversary! She stood under his window all night and cried

43

out, Avenge me of mine adversary! And he would not for a while. But after that day when this wild woman suddenly sprang in upon him with a knife hidden away among her rags—after that day he said, Because this widow troubleth me, I will avenge her, lest by her continual coming she weary me. There is a tinge of blood in the original ink that is lost in the tame translation, because there was a gleam of blood in the widow's eye on that last day of her warning and appeal to the unjust judge."[10]

The New Bible Commentary says that the argument of Jesus in 18:6-8 is this: "If an unrighteous judge will give a just judgment in the case of a helpless widow in whom he has no interest because of her ceaseless pleading, how much more will the holy God answer the unwearied cry for justice of His own chosen people? If He does not interpose to deliver them immediately, it is because He is long-suffering to their oppressors."[11]

The Speaker's Bible makes this explanation of Luke 18:8: "The parable was spoken to inculcate the necessity of persistent prayer with unabated confidence. . . . The question (of this verse) is, of course, a rhetorical one. Our Lord is not inquiring for information. But it is not, therefore, to be taken as a counterfeit one. Our Lord is not, in the form of a question, giving information. He neither expects to learn from His disciples, nor does He expect to teach them, by His question, whether such faith as He had been commending to them shall remain on the earth when He comes again. His object is to rouse to effort. What He is aiming at is ethical impression. He wishes to encourage His disciples to preserve that attitude of confident trust in God which it is the purpose of the parable to inculcate."[12]

George A. Buttrick makes his explanation picturesque: "There were only three ways of dealing with such a judge as is described; he could be bribed, bullied, or besought

44

until he surrendered. The widow had no wealth with which to bribe him, and no power with which to threaten. She could only plead with the persistence of despair. So she pleaded against hope. She entreated the judge at his tribunal. She waylaid him as he went home. Wherever he might go, there she would be, waiting to pour her intolerable tale of woe upon him. He could not escape her. At last, for his own comfort (he knew no law but his own gain) he did as she asked; it was the only way to be rid of her."[13]

The expository preacher should build a library of exegetical commentaries. Sermonic commentaries are useful but not as valuable as those that go down deep into the Hebrew and Greek Scriptures.

In the questionnaire survey we found the following use of commentaries:

72 used the *Pulpit Commentary*
70 used G. Campbell Morgan's expository works
70 used Matthew Henry's commentary
66 used *The Interpreter's Bible*
54 used Alexander Maclaren's *Expositions of Holy Scripture*
43 used *The Expositor's Greek New Testament*
41 used the works of A. T. Robertson
37 used *The Expositor's Bible*
35 used the works of Harry A. Ironside
24 used R. C. H. Lenski's commentaries
21 used *The International Critical Commentary*
14 used the commentaries of William Barclay
11 used Adam Clarke's commentary

As to modern English translations:

134 used *Phillips*
98 used the *American Standard Revised*

83 used the *Amplified New Testament*
77 used the *Revised Standard Version*
46 used *Weymouth*
44 used *Moffatt*
28 used *Williams*
20 used *Montgomery*
17 used the *Berkeley Version*
The *New English Bible* had just come off the press.

IV

Power Through

ORGANIZATION

BY DEFINITION A SERMON is an organized discourse. The better the organization, the better the sermon will probably be. If the preacher has applied the five processes recommended in gathering explanatory data regarding his text, he is now ready to think about the organization of his sermon. We believe that organization should come before argumentation, illustration, and application. If the preacher knows approximately what his outline is to be, he can arrange his arguments, illustrations and application in the most forceful locations.

Good organization has great value in marshaling the material of the sermon so that it is clear and persuasive to the listener; and it has just as much value to the preacher for it helps him to arrange his material in the best possible order and to remember it easily. The mind of the hearer searches for the key idea of the sermon and for the points to support it. If these are not evident, the listener feels frustrated in his listening effort and bewildered as to the thrust of the message. In our questionnaire on expository preaching, we found that seventy-eight out of the 223 responding said that organizing the expository sermon was a major problem to them.

Regarding the value of a good outline, G. Campbell Morgan wrote: "I believe that the preparation of the plan is of far more value than the writing of the sermon. The plan represents your thought, the composition your expression. . . . We should not try to build up the body of the sermon without the skeleton. It is a great advantage when we can see the skeleton—though we must not make that figure go on all fours. Let the people see the bones, the ribs, the great things that form the framework. I am far more concerned about that than about the verbiage."[1]

Also, Halford E. Luccock said, "The power of a sermon lies in its structure, not in its decoration."[2]

Harold J. Ockenga wrote: "Next to his theme, the outline is the most important step in the preparation of the sermon. The outline must express the original idea. Let it be fresh, new, individual, personal. . . . I spend more time on this step than on any other."[3]

What constitutes a good outline? Here is a condensation of the ideas of Ilion T. Jones: The outline should have unity, each point being a subthesis of the main thesis; it should have order, the points being co-ordinate; it should have proportion, all points being of parallel construction; it should have climax, the points being arranged in an ascending order. The wording should not be odd, smart or clever, but the points should be fresh, striking, and intriguing without being sensational.[4]

Often, otherwise good preachers do a poor job of outlining. Either they think anything will do, or they consider other parts of the sermonizing process more important, or they have never learned how to make an effective sermon outline.

Our main insistence is that the expository sermon outline be *vital, not wooden.* This idea comes from Harold C. Phillips in these words: "I think there is an advantage in not forcing an outline that does not come naturally, namely, this: an outline may be mechanical or organic,

48

wooden or vital. In a mechanical outline the three points are like three bricks, any three will do. A vital outline is like a tree—it has roots, trunk, limbs, branches, leaves."[5]

Two extra requirements for the expository sermon outline are that it must be true to its Scripture passage, and it must reveal the major ideas in the passage. This still leaves plenty of opportunity for originality and freshness.

In a wooden outline the points say little in themselves. They divide the material but they need explanation and elaboration in order to interest and challenge. In a vital outline the points deal with challenging truth of a timeless nature. The points themselves convey meaning and stimulate thought. We might illustrate the difference by comparing two diving boards at a swimming pool. One is long and springy. The divers bounce up and down on it until it thrusts them high into the air for a dive downward into the depths of the pool. The other is a stiff wooden beam without resiliency. It is only an unresponsive platform from which divers may push themselves off into the pool with a splash. The vital sermon point is like the springy board giving a big push into thought, while the wooden point is like the stiff beam from which one must push himself.

The *interrogative outline* is wooden. It asks such interrogative questions as: What? When? Where? How? Why? What then? Suppose you are preaching on Ruth's decision in Ruth 1:15-18, planning to involve the whole book as context. An interrogative outline would divide the material for you and raise questions for you to answer, but that is all. It would run something like this:

   I. What was the decision?
   II. Why was it made?
   III. Who made it?

IV. What did it cost?

V. What were the results?

This outline is commonplace. Anyone can create it without trying. It stirs no interest. The preacher's work is still to be done. What about a vital outline on this passage? Maybe you could take the theme, "The rewards of right decision," and you could say, "We see four rewards of a right decision in this book":

I. Refuge, 2:12

II. Rest, 3:1, 18

III. Redemption, 4:1-11

IV. Renown, 4:13-22[6]

You could adopt it and preach like an evangelist with this outline whereas the first would cause struggle and travail.

Look at Romans 3:27-31. You might use the theme, "Righteousness by faith," and ask,

I. What is it?

II. Why is it?

III. What does it do?

W. H. Griffith Thomas uses this thesis and outline, "God's righteousness is independent of the law or anything man can do."

I. Righteousness by faith excludes boasting, vv.27-28

II. Righteousness by faith is equally suited to all, vv.29-30

III. Righteousness by faith establishes the law, v.31[7]

Thomas' outline cries out for you to preach on it. Go ahead and preach it.

If you were preaching on Romans 5:1-11, your subject would be "Justification," and your outline, by the interrogative method, might be:

    I. What is justification?
   II. What are its blessings?
  III. When do we have them?

Harold J. Ockenga handles it better. Under the title, "The glorious benefits of being right with God," he discusses four benefits:

    I. We have peace toward God
   II. We have access to grace
  III. We rejoice in hope of glory
  IV. We shall be saved through His life[8]

When W. G. Coltman preached on Galatians 2:20, he might have handled it interrogatively under the theme, "The Victorious Life":

    I. What is this victorious life?
   II. Who can live it?
  III. When may it be lived?
  IV. How is it related to Christ?

But instead of this dull and wooden approach, he used the thesis, "This life involves three wonderful secrets":

    I. Christ instead of me
   II. Faith instead of feeling
  III. "Now" instead of "then"[9]

If we turn to the passage examined in the previous chapter, we could try the interrogative method of outlining it. Our theme might be, "The Praying Widow":

I. Why did the widow pray?
II. How did she pray?
III. What resulted?
IV. What lessons for us?

Maclaren combines it with the following parable of the Pharisee and the publican, Luke 18:1-14, under the title, "Three Kinds of Praying":

I. The wearisome widow and the unrighteous judge
II. The Pharisee and the publican[10]

In spite of his homiletical genius, this outline lacks impact.

J. C. Ryle discusses our passage in four and one half pages and puts his points, as he usually does, in the form of lessons:

I. The great importance of perseverance in prayer
II. God has an elect people upon the earth who are under His special care
III. True faith will be found very scarce at the end of the world[11]

George A. Buttrick combines this parable with that of the friend at midnight, Luke 11:5-13, for one sermon on "The God Who Answers Prayer." After five pages of stimulating explanatory discussion, he seems to use these as his main points, though they are not clearly marked:

I. Jesus regarded prayer as the simple outpouring of human need
II. Prayer must become a tireless beseeching before God can richly reward it
III. Our prayers must be freed of insincerity and the trivial spirit before heaven's bounty is unlocked

IV. Prayer is the central and determining force of a man's life[12]

The outlines above by Ryle and Buttrick avoid the interrogative pattern and deal in the realm of timeless, universal truths, and, therefore, they are more stimulating and preachable, though not couched in parallel phrasing.

W. B. Riley deals with Luke 18:6-8 as a text under the title, "Christ's Coming and the Eclipse of Faith." He says, "... the concluding sentence of this parable holds its most important truths":

    I. The certainty of the Second Coming
    II. The occasion of the Second Coming
    III. The query concerning the Second Coming[13]

This outline takes a topical approach to the text rather than an expository.

The Pulpit Commentary suggests an outline based on the idea of three contrasts in the passage:

    I. God in contrast with human avenger
    II. God's people in contrast with the widow
    III. The long-suffering of God in contrast with the long-suffering of man[14]

This is a vital outline and has preaching possibilities.

The Preacher's Complete Homiletic Commentary on the New Testament gives three outlines that could be reworked and used. Wells deals with the idea that men ought always to pray:

    I. The helpless
    II. The helper
    III. The appeal
    IV. The encouragements[15]

Miller, emphasizing the idea of continuing in prayer, calls us to keep in mind that

    I. God always hears the true prayer
   II. The reason of God's delay may be to increase our earnestness
  III. Many prayers are never answered because men faint at God's delay[16]

Arnot uses the title, "The Conditions of Importunate Prayer":

     I. Sense of need
    II. Desire to get
   III. Belief that God has in store what we desire
   IV. Belief that though He withholds awhile, He loves to be asked
    V. Belief that asking will obtain[17]

Spurgeon gives us a detailed and suggestive outline, using Luke 18:8 as his text, under the title, "The Search for Faith." He discusses the impressive features of his text:

    I. Remarkable if we consider the person mentioned as searching for faith
      1. When Jesus comes He will look for precious faith
      2. He will do so in His most sympathetic character
      3. The Son of man is the most likely person to discover faith if it is to be found
      4. Faith always looks to Christ
      5. The Son of man will give a wise and generous judgment in the matter
      6. Notice the time of scrutiny
      7. Notice the breadth of the region of search

II. It is exceedingly instructive in connection with the parable of which it is a part
    1. When the Son of man comes, shall He find upon earth the faith which prays importunately as this widow did?
    2. The importunate widow wailed with strong resolve, and never ceased through sullen doubt
    3. The widow staked her all upon the result of her pleading with the judge

III. Our text is suggestive in view of its form
    1. It warns us not to dogmatize about what the latter days will be
    2. This question leads us to much holy fear as to the matter of faith
    3. Many processes are in vigorous action which tend to destroy faith
    4. In addition, are there not influences which dwarf and stunt faith?
    5. Does not this invite us to intense watchfulness over ourselves?

IV. My text is very impressive in respect to personal duty
    1. Let faith have a home in our hearts
    2. Hold on to the Holy Scriptures as a great source of faith
    3. Make certain that you are born of the Holy Spirit, for you cannot have faith otherwise
    4. Believe in the precious blood of Christ shed for your sins
    5. Never relax your confidence in the efficacy of prayer, for the widow used no other weapon than prayer in her importunity with the judge
    6. Believe up to the hilt. Plunge into this sea of holy confidence in God and you shall find waters to swim in[18]

Spurgeon's outline is vital but goes considerably beyond

the scope of his text. His habit of making practical suggestions is evident. The sermon plan is partly expository, but
is also partly topical and textual.

To conclude this review of outlines on Luke 18:1-8, the
author presents two of his own outlines. They both deal
with the passage from the viewpoint of the praying widow
and are quite similar. The first is entitled, "End-time Praying," and uses the thesis, "This widow's praying reveals
four standards for all praying":

       I. She prayed persistently, v.3
      II. She prayed definitely, v.3
    III. She prayed earnestly, vv.3,5
    IV. She prayed believingly, vv. 3-7[19]

The second outline, under the title "Power in Prayer,"
says, "This widow continued to pray and did not faint, or
give up. When we analyze this story, we find that her praying had five characteristics":

       I. She prayed perseveringly, vv.3-5
      II. She prayed publicly, vv.3-6
    III. She prayed pointedly, v.3
    IV. She prayed pathetically, vv.3-7
     V. She prayed prevailingly, vv.5-8[20]

These outlines are expository, simple, clear, stimulating,
deal in timeless truths, and can be easily elaborated.
Though the second has one more main point, it is a little
better because the points are alliterative, and slightly more
specific and picturesque. See our third outline on this passage in the chapter on preparation.

Certain types of *analytical outlines* are also wooden. The
analysis consists of general terms that really substitute for
interrogatives. Note this outline by Walter T. Conner on
I John 4:7-21 under the title, "The Obligation to Love":

I. The source of love
II. The manifestation of love
III. The reproduction of love
IV. The perfecting of love[21]

While these points are clear, comprehensive, and in parallel construction, they deal with: *Where* do we get love? *How* do we recognize it? *What* does it do? *How* do we complete it? The points in themselves do not answer the questions raised. That must await their development. But the next outline by Conner becomes vital. It deals with I John 5:1-12 under the title, "Faith in the Son of God," by the thesis, "There are set out in this passage four things about faith in the Son of God:"

I. Faith in Jesus as the Christ is evidence of the new birth
II. Faith gives victory over the world
III. This faith is in response to the testimony of God to His Son
IV. Faith in the Son of God brings eternal life[22]

Each of these points says something vital about the passage under study.

Charles Simeon has a wooden outline on I Thessalonians 5:1-8. He uses the somewhat dull title, "Watchfulness Enjoined." After one and one half pages of explanation, he says, "We shall therefore speak of death and judgment as, in effect, the same to us; and we shall notice in succession":

I. The uncertainty of the period when death shall arrive
II. The character of those who are prepared for it
III. The duty of all in reference to it[23]

He then proceeds to restate each point and discuss it; of course, Simeon's expository volumes are not supposed to be full sermons, but only briefs of sermons. However, they do contain full outlines. While this particular outline states important ideas that are capable of expansion, it does so in a wooden way.

However, some of Simeon's outlines are vital and not wooden. For example, notice outline 2157 on Colossians 1:9-13. This he entitles, "Prayer for Growth in Grace," saying, ". . . he tells them what he prayed for on their behalf. He desired that they might advance":

    I. In the knowledge of God's will
   II. In obedience to His commands
  III. In the enjoyment of His presence
  IV. In submission to His dispensations
   V. In thankfulness to Him for His mercies[24]

This outline could undoubtedly be improved, but it has the virtues of dealing with timeless truths and practical responsibilities, then stating them in somewhat parallel construction. It is firmly rooted in the passage he discusses and has unity, clarity and simplicity.

The *mere contents outline* is usually wooden. It is another form of the analytical outline. One could take I Corinthians 13 as his text and use the title, "The Excellency of love demonstrates its excellency":

    I. The necessity of love, vv.1-3
   II. The evidences of love, vv.4-7
  III. The endurance of love, vv.8-13

This outline divides the material and suggests areas of discussion, but each point must be unfolded before there is challenge and interest. The writer uses this same title with the lead sentence, "Let us notice three ways by which love demonstrates its excellency":

I. Love makes life's gifts profitable, vv.1-3
II. Love makes life's relationships beautiful, vv.4-7
III. Love makes life's contributions eternal, vv.8-13[25]

In addition to parallel construction, each point in this last outline states a timeless, universal truth with vitality.

John A. Broadus has an expository sermon on John 4:32-38 with the title, "Some Laws of Spiritual Work." Using the thesis, "Now, from this passage with its images, I have wished to discourse upon some laws of spiritual work," he lists four points:

I. Spiritual work is refreshing to soul and body
II. There are seasons in the spiritual sphere—sowing seasons and reaping seasons
III. Spiritual work links the workers in unity
IV. Spiritual work has rich rewards[26]

This is a vital outline, stemming directly from the text and unfolding the passage satisfactorily and interestingly.

The best guarantee of sound sermonic organization lies in using the theme-thesis-key-word system of outlining. Every passage has a subject, a broad, general concept such as prayer, faith, hope, peace. Any subject can be broken down into themes or narrower concepts: the source of faith, the nature of faith, the power of faith, the loss of faith. Every passage will suggest several themes. The preacher selects the one that suits his purpose best, and narrows it still more into a thesis. The thesis adds a predicate to the theme, making it an affirmation, an interrogation, or an exhortation. If the theme were "the power of faith," the thesis might be, "Christians should experience the power of faith," or "How many Christians experience the power of faith?"

The thesis breaks down into main points, or divisions, by

applying one of the interrogatives: Why? How? When? Where? What? Who? If we apply the interrogative, How? to the first thesis above, we get the key words, "Ways," "Methods," "Processes," or other synonyms. Every main point must be a way of experiencing the power of faith, but each point must be taught in the passage being expounded. Let us suppose that the main points are obtained:

I. Through study of the Word of God
II. Through faithful prayer to God
III. Through service for the people of God

Each point is separate and distinct, yet vitally related to each other through the key word.

The thesis (sometimes called the proposition, the central statement, the controlling assertion, or the hinge of the sermon) is the integrating center of the sermon. It is the sermon in a nutshell, the whole sermon condensed into one sentence. J. H. Jowett always worked hard to obtain the best phrasing of this central statement.

The thesis should be a generalization conveying a timeless, universal truth, in a simple sentence, important enough to be worthy of unfolding into a sermon. But the thesis must be taught in the text. The purpose of the thesis is to clarify what the sermon is about, to unify its thoughts, and to simplify the discussion. The didactic thesis simply lays down an important affirmation to be proved or explained in the outline; the sermonic thesis lays responsibility on the listeners by incorporating the words, "You should," "You ought," or "You must." The interrogative thesis is in the form of a question to be answered by the main points. The hortatory thesis is an exhortation in the form of "Let us ...," or "Make certain ..." or some such phrase.

The key word is not the subject word, the theme word, or the central word of the main idea; it is a plural noun telling what the main points are. Such plural nouns as reasons, ways, steps, stages, areas, answers, assurances, directives, incentives, visions, are key words. We use only one key word in a single outline.

The key word has seven values: 1) to classify, label, or catalogue the main points, keeping them all in one category; 2) to point the direction you intend to follow with your thesis; 3) to give unity to the sermon; 4) to aid in parallel construction of main points; 5) to test the main points proving whether or not they fit the outline; 6) to link the main points together, tying them into a neat bundle; 7) to make the sermon easier to memorize and easier for the hearers to remember.

This system may seem mechanical and rigid, and it is, but not offensively so. But it saves time and helps the preacher do a better job of sermonic organization. It gives that power in organization which we seek. A fuller discussion of it will be found in Chapter 5 of *Variety in Your Preaching*, by Perry and Whitesell.

Various ways of outlining, some of them clever and unique, are demonstrated by H. E. Luccock in Chapter 13 of *In the Minister's Workshop*, and in Chapter 6 of *Principles and Practices of Preaching*, by Ilion T. Jones, but they cannot all be applied to expository preaching.

V

Power Through

ARGUMENTATION

NOT AS MUCH EMPHASIS is put upon formal argument in preaching as was done a few generations ago. Older books on preaching written by Broadus, Phelps, Pattison, and Breed contained chapters on argument. But recent writers such as Blackwood, Luccock, Sangster, Davis, and Jones hardly mention it. David R. Breed, in 1911, noticed this shift: "The older books upon homiletics gave a very large place to the consideration of argumentation; some of them devoted chapter after chapter to the subject. Various forms of argument were considered, one after another, with minute care and large emphasis, but it is a most significant fact that the books upon preaching in its various forms which have appeared within the past few years contain scarcely a reference to the subject."[1]

Does this mean that argument is not as important in preaching as it used to be? In part, it does. People are not used to lengthy or heavy arguments today. They are swayed more by illustrations, humor and emotion than by sober argument. A century and more ago denominational rivalry was fierce. Preachers defended their own positions and attacked those of other denominations with strong arguments. Sometimes outstanding debaters conducted public debates on religious questions which lasted a week or more. They used the technicalities of argument cleverly and sharply. Such proceedings are not known today. We are more likely to hear of tolerance and the right to choose among religious positions according to one's own individual preference.

But there is still a place for argument in preaching, especially when we think of it as a means to persuasion. The concept of persuasion is a prominent one today. While argumentation proper is the use of reasoned discourse to get others to believe or to do what we think they should, we might enlarge this meaning to include all right methods in preaching to persuade people to do right. If so, argumentation and persuasion are much alike.

Breed had this idea: "Let it be remembered that suitable argumentation is no more or other than the art of persuasion. He who adopts it, particularly in the pulpit, for any other purpose, has misused it. Dr. Willis G. Craig . . . has said . . ., 'The problem of argumentation is to make use of the best means of bringing others to believe or act as we wish them to believe or act.' Consider how much such a principle involves. It rules out of argument everything calculated to arouse the antagonism of the opponent; everything that reflects on his motives; everything that ministers to pride or prejudice; everything that is associated with ridicule and sarcasm; everything that looks for personal victory and the glory of conquest. The principle confines the debater to those arguments and considerations which are likely to please and win our adversaries."[2]

T. H. Pattison believed that, from the viewpoint of Scripture, argumentation in preaching has great importance: "Pictorial though it was, a strain of reasoning ran through the teaching of Jesus. When it was first preached by the apostles the gospel was preached argumentatively. Our faith in the great central truths of salvation rests on the basis of argument."[3]

Phillips Brooks said, "A sermon exists in and for its purpose. That purpose is the persuading and moving of men's souls,"[4] and John A. Broadus asserted: "Every preacher, then, ought to develop and discipline his powers in respect to argument. If averse to reasoning, he should constrain himself to practice it; if by nature strongly inclined that way, he must remember the serious danger of deceiving himself and others by false arguments . . . one must constantly remind himself to argue for truth rather than victory, and as a rule never to maintain a proposition which he does not really believe."[5]

In expository preaching formal arguments are usually few but the major methods of persuasion have a large place. Let us take ten methods of argumentation, or persuasion, in expository preaching.

The first, by *the use of the Word of God*. Since expository preaching gives first place to unfolding the meaning of the Scriptures (usually a rather large passage) the persuasive power of the Word of God comes into strong play. Broadus wrote: "The Scriptures themselves are an authority indeed. All that they testify to be fact is thereby fully proven, all that they teach as true and right is thereby established and made obligatory."[6]

Again, he said: "Argument in preaching has one peculiarity. There is a great authority, the Word of God, whose plain utterances upon any question must be held by the preacher as decisive and final. This is proof without arguing in the narrow sense."[7]

Part of the power in evangelist Billy Graham's preaching lies in his frequent use of "The Bible says. . . ." He believes that whether or not men believe the Bible to be the Word of God, there is an authority and persuasive power in it that cannot be ignored.

When we accept what the Bible says about itself, we

65

see that it claims strong persuasive power. Please note the following:

It converts (revives, RSV) the soul (Psalm 19:7, KJV)

It accomplishes the divine purpose (Isaiah 55:11, KJV)

It is like a fire and like a hammer that breaks the rock in pieces (Jeremiah 23:29, KJV)

It is as seed sown in the soil of men's hearts (Matthew 13:23, KJV)

If it cannot persuade men to repent, neither will one come back from the dead (Luke 16:31, KJV)

The words of Jesus are spirit and life (John 6:63, KJV)

The word of grace is able to build up and to give an inheritance among the sanctified (Acts 20:32, KJV)

It is the sword of the Spirit (Ephesians 6:17, KJV)

It is living and active, sharper than any two-edged sword, piercing to the division of soul and spirit, of joints and marrow, and discerning the thoughts and intentions of the heart (Hebrews 4:12, KJV)

It is inspired of God and profitable for teaching, for reproof, for correction, and for training in righteousness, that the man of God may be complete, equipped for every good work (II Timothy 3:16—17, RSV)

The second persuasive factor is *the character of the preacher.* Aristotle called this the "ethos," meaning the impression the speaker makes upon his audience. People certainly expect an expository preacher to be a man who not only knows and believes the Book, but also one who lives the Book. They wish to believe that back of everything he says is the fact that he is a man of God. James H. McBurney, James M. O'Neill, and Glen E. Mills tell us that in the area of secular argumentation and debate the ethos of the advocate should include assurance, preparation, intensity, flexibility, sincerity, directness, and modesty when referring to himself.[8] All these and more should character-ize the expository preacher. The very fact that the exposi-tor lives much in study and meditation upon the Scriptures should go far to make him a holy man.

The third method of argumentation is *reasoning*. Aris-totle named this "logos." This means the use of logic and formal methods of argument. Paul made frequent use of reasoning as these references show:

In Athens, he spent three weeks reasoning or arguing (rsv) with them out of the Scriptures (Acts 17:2, kjv)

In the same city, he disputed or argued (rsv) in the synagogue with the Jews and the devout persons, and in the market place every day (Acts 17:17, kjv)

In Corinth, he reasoned or argued (rsv) in the synagogue every sabbath and persuaded Jews and Greeks (Acts 18:4)

In Ephesus, he went into the synagogue and argued with the Jews (Acts 18:19, rsv)

Again, in Ephesus, "And he entered the synagogue and for three months spoke boldly, arguing and pleading about the kingdom of God" (Acts 19:8, rsv). From the synagogue, he moved to the hall of Tyrannus and argued daily (19:9, rsv)

The same Greek word for reasoning or arguing is used of Paul's preaching in Troas (Acts 20:7, kjv) and of his presentation to Felix and Drusilla (Acts 24:25, rsv)

In addition to argument from the testimony of Scripture, there is general argument from testimony, analogy, cause to effect, effect to cause, induction and deduction, and from examples. When explanation is done well it has per-suasive effect.

The fourth persuasive element is *the emotional appeal*. Aristotle referred to this as "pathos," or appeal to the feel-ings. We should never appeal to emotion for its own sake but for the sake of moving men to positive action. Most people are more likely to be moved by their emotions than by their reason. We should never appeal to baser motives but we may rightly appeal to higher ones. Broadus reduces them to three: happiness, holiness and love.

Charles W. Koller has treated them as the seven appeals to the heart: the appeal to altruism, the appeal to aspiration, the appeal to curiosity, the appeal to duty, the appeal to fear, the appeal to love, the appeal to reason.[9] In no case is the emotional appeal to be separated from the appeal to reason.

A fifth persuasive element is *the use of facts and statistics.* Blackwood is strong on the use of facts in preaching. This is a day of statistics. Batteries of computers spew them out; mountains of records and filing cabinets preserve them; the magazines and newspapers publicize them. While very few people remember the statistics they hear or read, they tend to be swayed by them.

If the preacher can cite statistics to show that Sunday school pupils become less involved in crime than others, he has a strong argument for Sunday school attendance. If he can prove by statistics that divorce is more common among unbelievers than believers, he has a strong case. Walter A. Maier packed his sermons with relevant statistics and facts.

A sixth consideration in persuasion is *audience analysis.* This means finding out the facts about his congregation and about the physical factors under which he preaches. The preacher should know his audience's age range, educational range, occupations, cultural interests, prejudices, sex division, and spiritual maturity. In addition, if he knows something about the homes of his people, the institutions in the community, the history of the area, and the traditions of the neighborhood, he will be better prepared to speak to them. Of course, he should know the seating conditions of the sanctuary, the acoustics, and the ventilation and lighting facilities. These are areas of knowledge which an alert pastor will soon gain as he lives in a community and mingles with its people. But it is easy to take some of these items for granted and not be really informed about them.

After a period of acquaintance, it would be wise for a pastor to take inventory of his congregation. This could be done by passing out a card or check-sheet listing items for checking, but requiring no signature. One might be a Bible knowledge inventory, another a spiritual achievement inventory. One could be a Christian literature inventory, another a Christian aspiration inventory. If the people were taken into partnership, by showing them that they were helping their pastor to preach more effectively and to serve them better, they would not object to checking a few audience inventory records.

An important modern emphasis in preaching is that of preaching to the needs of the people. This can be done as well in expository preaching as any other, maybe better. But we must know what the needs of the people are. It is the purpose of audience analysis to determine them.

The seventh method of persuasion is *visualization.* This means that we try to picture the new life in such a way that the listener sees himself living it. In the case of the unconverted, the approach might be: "Picture how much better off you would be now if you were a Christian. You would know forgiveness of sins, the power of prayer, the guidance of the Holy Spirit, and happy fellowship with God's people."

If the appeal were to urge people to become tithers, you might say: "Let us think how it would go with you if you were a tither. You would have so much money to give to your church that you would be glad to come and put it on

69

the offering plate. You would feel a sense of partnership with our work here and in the mission fields of the world much more than you experience now. Can you not see yourself enjoying the other nine tenths that you have left for yourself much more than if you were trying to squeeze out a little for God while you stretch the rest to cover the bills?"

Alan H. Monroe's famous motivated sequence consists of five steps in persuasive speeches:

1. The attention step—getting attention
2. The need step—showing the need
3. The satisfaction step—showing how to satisfy the need
4. The visualization step—visualizing the results
5. The action step—requesting action or approval

Of the visualization step, he says, "The visualization step should project the audience into the future so that they are emotionally impressed with an image of future conditions."[10]

The eighth element of argumentation in expository preaching is *testimony*, already mentioned under reasoning. This refers to accounts of personal experience which support the Scripture passage expounded. The testimony of the preacher himself will carry considerable weight, but it cannot be used often. The experiences of members of his family will bear using occasionally.

A preacher should keep a file of conversion experiences told in the words of the convert. Other personal accounts of answers to prayer, the guidance of the Holy Spirit, physical healing, solutions to problems, deeper experiences, divine deliverances, and personal evangelism cases can all be used to illustrate various points in expository sermons.

The man who reads Christian biography will find many illustrations in the area of testimony. The pastor who visits among his people will hear many testimonies of God's help which he can feel free to use. This will not be true in most of his counseling cases.

The expository preacher will use the testimonies of the Bible characters themselves when they support a point. The conversion cases of Paul, Lydia, and the Philippian jailor are ones that can often be used.

David R. Breed calls testimony the best argument: "It is well, however, to emphasize the argument from testimony as generally the best for the preacher's use. Testimony is involved in every other form of argumentation. It is virtually inseparable from it. There can be no proof without evidence. Testimony is witness borne to a fact. . . . This argument is, therefore, more frequently employed in the Scripture than any other, as much perhaps as all other forms of argument put together, both in the Old Testament and in the New. The God of the Scripture appeals to his witnesses and calls upon them for their testimony."[11]

The ninth method in effective argumentation is *answering objections*. Since the preacher's audience seldom has an opportunity to voice questions or objections during the meeting, it is no more than fair and courteous for the preacher to try to anticipate some of them. In doing so he will try to state them with force and fairness, and proceed to give his answer. This tends to cut the ground from under an objector before he can firmly claim it.

During the preparation of his message, the preacher can look at it from the known viewpoints of members of his congregation, asking himself what objections they might have to his interpretations and applications. Paul used this form of argument in: Acts 26:25-29; Romans 3:5-9, 31; 6:1-4; 9:19-21.

In anticipating objections, the preacher will seek to avoid two mistakes. First, he will not raise objections that no one has; that would only be a waste of time. Second, when he does anticipate objections, he will show respect and consideration for those who might hold them. He will not ridicule, lambaste, or be sarcastic toward the imaginary objector and his question.

If the preacher has done a good job of audience analysis, he will understand what objections his people might have to certain doctrines or interpretations of Scripture. And if he lives in close touch with his people, he will meet many objections in one form or another.

Excuses for not believing and obeying the gospel are probably easier to anticipate than are objections. Certainly there is much practical value in foreseeing and answering them with Christian grace and kindliness. Moses had plenty of excuses in Exodus 3-4, and so did people in Jesus' day, Luke 14:16-24.

The tenth method of persuasion is *good arrangement*. When the sermon outline is orderly, logical, and cumulative, it becomes persuasive. The persuasive element can be made stronger if the thesis contains a responsibility word: "You should," "You ought," or "You must."

Walter A. Maier, formerly of the "Lutheran Hour," has a sermon on John 3:5-7, entitled, "Be Born Again in Christ." He discusses his thesis under this outline:

I. You need the new birth
II. You must have the new birth to be saved
III. You can have the new birth[12]

F. W. Robertson's sermon on Mark 14:41-42 has a simplicity, clarity and force that is persuasive. The text reads: "And he cometh the third time, and saith unto them, Sleep on now, and take your rest: it is enough, the hour is come; behold, the Son of man is betrayed into the hands of sinners. Rise up, let us go; lo, he that betrayeth me is at hand" (KJV).

Robertson uses the title, "The Irreparable Past," and has two main points: the irreparable past and the available future. Under the second main point he says: "Youth has its irreparable past. And therefore, my young brethren, let it be impressed upon you—*NOW* is a time, infinite in its value for eternity, which will never return again. Sleep not; learn that there is a very solemn work of heart which must be done while the stillness of the garden of your Gethsemane gives you time. Now—or never."[13]

His concluding sentences are: "There is a past which is gone forever. But there is a future which is still our own."[14]

Two other important factors in persuasion are competent sermon delivery and the power of the Holy Spirit; these are considered in later chapters.

VI
Power Through
ILLUSTRATION

A SERMON IS VIRTUALLY worthless without good illustrations. We live in an increasingly visual-minded generation. If an article in a magazine or newspaper is not accompanied by photographs or drawings, many readers will not notice it, let alone read it. This carries over into preaching.

Illustrations are the photographs or pictures that go along with abstract ideas. Donald G. Smith claims that illustrations in a sermon may serve any one or more of the following purposes: gain interest, throw light on the subject, clarify the subject, make truth vivid, strengthen argument, bring conviction, aid persuasion, make for lasting impressions, give the sermon splendor, allow for the injection of humor, lend itself to variety, stimulate the imagination of the audience, permit the speaker to speak indirectly, appeal to all classes of people, help to make a good conclusion.[1]

Psychology claims that we learn about eighty-five per cent through sight, about ten per cent through hearing, about two per cent through touch, about one and one half per cent through smell, and about one and one half per cent through taste. This would certainly argue strongly for making sermonic material as vivid or picturesque as reasonably possible.

Expository preaching must embody a large amount of explanation and application. These two elements tend to be abstract. Therefore, we need illustrations. On the other hand, the expository sermon will probably not have as much space to give to illustrations as topical or textual sermons do. If expository sermons deal with narrative and action events in the Scriptures, and if the preacher uses his imagination to build up and present his material, the outside illustrations can be very few. But if he is dealing with doctrinal and didactic Biblical matter, he should use more illustrations.

In our questionnaire survey, ninety-four out of 223 pastors had a major problem finding good illustrations for expository sermons. This may have included most of those who claimed to be expository preachers, for only one hundred out of the 223 said that expository preaching predominated in their preaching programs. Sources of illustrations for the pastors reporting were:

1. The Bible: 181
2. Experience: 180
3. Observation: 117
4. Newspapers and magazines: 102
5. Conversations: 54
6. Imagination: 53
7. Biographies: 51
8. Their files: 43
9. Radio and TV: 32
10. Books of illustrations: 20
11. Literature and history: 5

Let us consider some of these sources and give some examples. The Bible rightly stands first as a contributor of expository sermon illustrations. In the foreword to his book, *Evangelistic Illustrations from the Bible,* this author wrote in part as follows:

Evangelicals commonly agree that illustrations from the Bible are the best and that we should all use more of them than we do. Biblical illustrations have many advantages over others: they teach the Word; they honor the God of the Bible; they enlist the presence and power of the Holy Spirit; they open the

76

hearts and minds of hearers in unexpected ways; they give the speaker added authority; they never wear out; and they never arouse adverse criticism. . . . The author does not claim that all illustrations should come from the Bible, or that biblical illustrations are the only good ones. . . . Out of the total number of illustrations used in a message, perhaps half or more may profitably come from the Scriptures. For greatest effectiveness, Bible illustrations should be thoroughly studied and carefully fitted into the message. The historical imagination ought to be used freely in order to put life and freshness into biblical events.[2]

Each Biblical illustration can be used to shed light upon a number of truths. For example, take the story of Abraham offering his son Isaac at Mount Moriah, Genesis 22. This event illustrates faith, love, self-sacrifice, obedience, the way of salvation, the mercy of God, and God's attitude toward human sacrifice.

Personal experience rates almost as high as the Bible as a source of expository sermon illustrations. There can be no doubt about the power of personal experience illustrations. The speaker has participated, and his authority can hardly be questioned; he speaks with confidence and vividness. He must be careful not to use too many illustrations of this category in a single sermon or a single series, else he seems a braggart; and he must be watchful of his facts, so that he does not exaggerate and thus lose the confidence of his hearers. Notice how great expositors do it.

Harry A. Ironside had a vast fund of personal experiences and used them freely in his expository preaching. Hardly anyone could match him as a master user of personal experiences. Speaking on I Corinthians 6:11, "And such were some of you: but ye are washed, but ye are sanctified, but ye are justified in the name of the Lord Jesus, and by the Spirit of our God," he used this illustration:

77

I went into a mission in San Francisco years ago and sat for perhaps half-an-hour listening to marvelous testimonies of redeeming grace. One after another rose and painted a dreadful picture of his past life and then told how God had saved him. I had come to that meeting with a little sermon all made up, but as I sat listening to these testimonies, I said, "O dear, my stupid little sermon! To think I imagined I could go into my study and develop a little discourse that would suit a congregation like this, when I had no idea of the kind of people I was going to address." So I just "canned" my sermon; I put it out of my mind, and when I rose to speak, I took this text: "And such were some of you: but ye are washed, but ye are sanctified, but ye are justified in the name of the Lord Jesus, and by the Spirit of our God." It was easy to preach to them then without a lot of study. These sermons that you get up are so hard to preach, but those that come down are so much easier. At the close a dignified personage came to me and said, "Do you know, you got your theology terribly mixed tonight?"

"Did I?" I said. "Straighten me out."

"You put sanctification before justification. You have to be justified and then you get the second blessing."

"Pardon me, but you are mistaken," I said. "I did not put sanctification before justification."

"You most certainly did."

"I most certainly did not; it was the apostle Paul who did."

"Why, you cannot blame your wrong theology on him."

"I was simply quoting Scripture."

"You misquoted it. It reads, 'Ye are justified, ye are sanctified.'"

"No, no," I said; "read it."

And he began to read, "But ye are washed, but ye are sanctified, but ye are justified," and then he said, "Why, there is a misprint there. Wait a minute; I will get a Revised Bible."

He got it and looked at it, and read, "Washed, sanctified, justified."

"Why," he said, "I never saw that before; but all I have got

78

to say is the apostle Paul was not clear on the holiness question when he wrote that!"[3]

Let us not hesitate to use personal experience illustrations if they are modest and will do the job better than others. And, let us not feel that we have to beg pardon or apologize for using them. People do not feel embarrassed to use illustrations from personal experience in private conversation. Why should they in public proclamation?

Illustrations from *observation* can often be used. These have not been experienced but have been seen in nature or the experience of others. They stand next to personal experiences in effectiveness. J. H. Jowett, commenting on Philippians 1:12 about the furtherance of the gospel, wrote: "Some time ago, I saw a railway embankment on fire, and the mercilessly invading flames were, inch by inch, consuming every blade of grass upon the slope, until a great area was black in unrelieved destruction. Some weeks later I passed by the same place, but instead of the scarred and blackened ruins there was a wide patch of fresh and most winsome green. Where the fire had burnt most fiercely the recreated slope was the most attractive. 'The things that happened' unto it, 'had fallen out rather unto the progress' of vegetation. 'God is love,' and therefore He is 'a consuming fire.' "[4]

Note the choice use of words and the accurate application of this illustration from observation.

While we are thinking of Jowett, let us learn from him that illustrations can be very short. Here are some others from his volume on Philippians:

He (Paul) had a fine eye for the lineaments of grace, and he could discern the sproutings of holy desire, even when they were buried beneath the refuse of sin and long-continued negligence.[5]

79

He nourishes the tender sapling into the majestic oak, and the one gracious sunshine is showered upon both.[6]

We are always optimistic about the people who dwell in our hearts. When they only dwell in the suburbs of our regards we soon lose hope concerning them. . . .[7]

There is love which is as candle-light; there is love which is as steady starlight; and there is love which is as the glorious splendour of the noonday sun.[8]

Picnic weather does not reveal the sea-going powers of a liner; these are tested and made manifest by the tempest.[9]

Our prayers cut channels for the river of God's gracious Spirit.[10]

Marcus Dods uses historical imagination well in an illustrative capacity. He is discussing Jesus washing the feet of His disciples:

Instead of unmasking him (Judas), Jesus makes no difference between him and the others, kneels by his couch, takes his feet in His hands, washes and gently dries them.[11]

Shame and astonishment shut the mouths of the disciples, and not a sound broke the stillness of the room but the tinkle and splash of the water in the basin as Jesus went from couch to couch. But the silence was broken when He came to Peter.[12]

Jesus could very well have eaten with men who were unwashed; but He could not eat with men hating one another, glaring fiercely across the table, declining to answer or to pass what they were asked for, showing in every way malice and bitterness of spirit.[13]

Every expository sermon should draw illustrations from several sources. In W. B. Riley's sermon on I Thessalonians

5:1-20, "Preparation for the Second Appearance," he uses twelve brief pages, for seven major illustrations and one minor one. The major illustrations are: W. L. Pettingill—one page; a motorist picking up a hitchhiker—nearly one page; Moses—half a page; the Duke of Wellington—one third of a page; John Bradford—half a page; James Gilmour, half a page; Benjamin Franklin—half a page. The minor illustration is in the conclusion, about Emperor Tiberius, and uses five lines.[14]

It is often possible to get illustrations from the use of Greek or Hebrew words. A. T. Robertson's set on *Word Pictures in the New Testament* gives many examples.

J. D. Jones, speaking of the tears of Jesus, John 11:34-35, says: "The verb he used to describe the weeping of Mary is the word *klaio*, the verb he uses to describe the weeping of Jesus is the verb *dakriuo*. Now, the difference between the two verbs is something like this: *klaio* suggests loud and convulsive lamentation, sobbing, and wailing; *dakriuo* suggests the silent shedding of tears. Mary *wailed*. But of Jesus, the Evangelist only says that *tears fell from him*."[15]

Alexander Maclaren used quite a few very short illustrations, and hardly any long ones. Looking casually through his volume on Luke, chapters 13-24, we notice these:

. . . when wealth has flung its golden chains round so many professing Christians.[16]

Peter shoves his oar in, after his fashion.[17]

The Cross was flinging its shadow over him. He was bracing himself up for the last struggle.[18]

He would have trodden down all such flimsy obstacles as a lion "from the thickets of Jordan" crashes through the bulrushes, but this cry stopped Him, "Jesus, thou Son of David, have mercy on me."[19]

But when blind Bartimaeus cried, Jesus smiled down upon him —though his sightless eyeballs could not see the smile, there would be a smile in the cadence of His words. . . .[20]

If any poor, blind Bartimaeus remembers that, and asks accordingly, he has the key to the royal treasury in his possession, and he may go in and plunge his hand up to the wrist in jewels and diamonds, and carry away bars of gold, and it will all be his.[21]

G. Campbell Morgan seldom used stories and personal experiences for illustrations. He knew how to weigh and balance words and turn his Scripture material into illustrations. In his sermon on "The Unchanging One," Hebrews 13:8, we see these brief illustrations: "We need a center of permanence, not an anchorage. An anchorage means limitation and monotony. An anchorage belongs to a ship and is a hindrance to the ship. The tug of the ship to be away from the shore and out upon the sea is of its very nature and being, and the anchor holds it back. We are not asking for an anchorage."[22]

"We look to our friends, and the story is tragic. The air is full of farewells to the dying. We look to circumstances, and there is neither anchorage that holds nor freshness that satisfies the soul. Where are we? Great God! Where are we? We must find anchorage in that broader sense of the word somewhere. Where shall we turn?"[23]

In Morgan's sermon on "The Madness of Jesus," Mark 3:21, we find these vivid passages:

If you journey with Him imaginatively through the fields, and the walled-in town, and the country towns, and the great cities, you are impressed with the quiet self-possession of this Man; there seems to be no touch of insanity about Him.[24]

A sparrow falls and sickens and dies, and has as Comrade in its dying, God. When that man bending to his toil, overwhelmed with it, bearing the burden and heat of the day, wipes from his brow the sweat and dust of toil, and with it some hair of his head, God has numbered that hair![25]

The Pope of Rome said that Luther ought to be in bedlam. The men of his own church said Xavier was mad. All England laughed at the unutterable folly of John Wesley. Many people thought William Booth was not quite sane! It has run through the centuries.[26]

That little bit of work you did this afternoon does seem rather old-fashioned and out of date; that class of children that fidgeted all the while is just a little behind the times, is it not? A thousand times No! That is building for eternity and hastening the coming of the Kingdom of God. That call you made that no one knows about save you and the sick one, the flowers you took, the word of cheer, the tender approach to a soul that asked how it was between that soul and God; all that is Christly work.[27]

But let us not undervalue the foolish, simple, wandering, restless methods; the method that does things as they come and never draws up a program. That is the whole story of the life and ministry of Jesus. He did things as He went, as He passed by, as He went out, as He was by the sea. In the midst of preaching somebody disturbed Him, and He halted His preaching and went after Jairus; and on the way with Jairus a woman touched Him, and He left Jairus on one side to attend to the woman that went on again. He did the next thing that came, because to those eyes the Kingdom was ever present. That touch of the hand, that glance of the eye, and that tone of the voice, all spoke of it and brought its power nearer. He was content to wait, as He still is waiting, till His enemies be made the footstool of His feet.[28]

Pictorial preaching such as this does not need to be bolstered up by anecdotes, stories and personal experiences. There is such vividness, movement, color, and dramatic power about it that it holds interest and challenges thought without further illustrative material. But Morgan did sometimes use a poem, or a pointed story such as this one: "He received sinners; sat down at the table and ate with them. He was the friend of publicans and sinners. Let me tell you what so eminent a scholar as Dr. Bruce once said about this. Speaking to Mr. Samuel Chadwick, he said, 'You know, Chadwick, that word "friend" is not good enough; it does not really catch the meaning of the word behind it.' Mr. Chadwick looked at him and said, 'What would you put there?' 'Well,' he said, 'the fact of the matter is, the only word that catches it is the word the boys use—"chum."' He is the chum of publicans and sinners. I tell you who said that as you might object to it if I said it."[29]

F. B. Meyer created illustrations by the use of his historical imagination. Speaking of Moses' mother, he paints this picture:

She was not always on the qui vive for the step of officer or midwife. She would take all ordinary precaution; but she would never give way to excessive fear. Sometimes when her heart grew sick she would betake herself to her knees, and plead the Divine promise on which she had been caused to hope. The whole family lived on that woman's faith, as men live on bread; and God's angels bent over the unconscious babe, shielding it with their tenderest care, and whispering their love-words into its ear. Finally, the mother was led by the good Spirit of God to weave the papyrus rushes into a little ark, or boat, coating it

84

with bitumen, to make it impervious to wet. There she put the child with many a kiss, closed the lid upon its sweet face, with her own hands bore it to the water's edge, and placed it tenderly among the flags that grew there.[30]

It all befell according to the mother's faith. The princess, accompanied by a train of maidens, came to the river bank to bathe. She saw the ark among the flags, and sent her maid to fetch it. In the midst of the little group the lid was carefully uplifted; and their eyes were charmed with the sight of the beautiful face, whilst their hearts were touched with the whimper of the babe, who missed its mother, and was frightened by its unwonted surroundings and the many strange faces.[31]

A beautiful example of building up an event, in its own geographical setting, into a vivid illustration is this one from Meyer concerning Moses and the burning bush, Exodus 3:

Quite ordinary was that morning as it broke. The sun rose as usual in a dull haze over the expanse of sand, or above the gaunt forms of the mountains, seamed and scarred. As the young day opened, it began to shine in a cloudless sky, casting long shadows over the plains; and presently, climbing to the zenith, threw a searching, scorching light into every aperture of the landscape beneath. The sheep browsed as usual on the scant herbage, or lay panting beneath the shadow of a great rock; but there was nothing in their behaviour to excite the thought that God was nigh. The giant forms of the mountains, the spreading heavens, the awful silence unbroken by the song of bird or hum of insect life, the acacia bushes drooping in the shadeless glare—these things were as they had been for forty years, and as they threatened to be, after Moses had sunk into an obscure and forgotten grave. Then, all suddenly, a common bush began to shine with the emblem of Deity; and from its heart of fire the voice of God broke the silence of the ages in

85

words that fell on the shepherd's ear like a double-knock: "Moses, Moses."[32]

On the expository preaching scene today is Harold J. Ockenga. He uses variety in his sermon illustrations, including personal experiences, for which he does not apologize. In his sermon on "The Growth of a Church," based on I Thessalonians 1:2-4, he uses the thesis, "What were the factors in this growth in grace?" This is followed by a simple, alliterative, three-point outline:

     I. Prayer
    II. Progress
   III. Predestination

We find him using these illustrations:

The concept of grace was the predominant thought in the ministry of John Henry Jowett. His biographer, Arthur Porritt, says, "To Jowett, redeeming grace was the fulcrum of the evangelical message. . . . In a hundred sermons he proclaimed it. All his wealth of imagery and illustration was lavished upon this theme."[33]

I have often felt, as a pastor, that I made a mistake in so abruptly breaking off relationships to my previous church, which I had served for five and one-half years. Under the mistaken notion that I ought to leave the field free for my successor, I refused to have much intercourse with the members and friends of that church by means of mail and personal visit. Had I to do it over again, I would not have pursued that course any more than St. Paul withdrew all interest in the Thessalonian Church when he left that community.[34]

From time to time God has privileged me to be used in sending young men into the ministry. Recently a letter came stating the

86

source and strength and comfort which my own evangelical position has been to a young man now in a pulpit of great prominence. I pray God that stability and strength will always be mine so that those who have been led into the ministry because of my own influence will find comfort and courage in it.[35]

I count as my personal friends many of the greatest living leaders of the church, who are likewise loyal to the faith of Jesus Christ.[36]

Here was a helpless church without teachers, without written Bible, without past experience, and without knowledge. No wonder Paul was concerned about their continuance in the faith. No wonder he prayed for them constantly.[37]

Several such experiences I too have known under the blessing and grace of God. One was the Mid-Century Evangelistic Campaign when the Lord did so graciously a great work in Massachusetts and in New England. Another was at St. John, New Brunswick, where a whole series of churches could not contain the people who wanted to hear the gospel and where scores and scores accepted Christ in a few days. What God has done once, He can do again.[38]

Let past blessings excite faith for future ones. This is the value of keeping a prayer list. As you mark the answers to your previous prayers, you have faith to ask God for greater things to come.[39]

Some men of prayer found it essential to pray while they were kneeling, others while they were lying on their faces, but talk to Him they did. I know a man of God who also is well known to you all who usually begins on his knees and before he finishes in prayer will have walked up and down the room and finally have fallen on his face before God.[40]

At Wesley's home on City Road, London, one may see the room where he slept for the last eighteen years of his life. Opening off that room to the east is a little closet with a fireplace and a window. In it is a table and a chair and a candlestick. Here is where John Wesley prayed an hour each morning for his churches, his local preachers, his converts, his sermons, and all the phases of the Wesleyan Revival. When the sun came up in the east, John Wesley was on his knees in prayer.[41]

Everyone wants to be remembered and memory is a wonderful aid to prayer and good works. When an aged parent becomes feebleminded and irresponsible, many a child who has locked up the closet of memory puts such a parent away, whereas he who will remember the works of love, of provision, of faith, and of sacrifice made by that parent will be led into good works in caring for him.[42]

The tree must not only have the trunk and branches, but a root system which compares in size to the trunk and the branches. Faith is the root; works are the fruit.[43]

Christians have been noted for taking upon themselves such redemptive labors which are exhausting. Probably two of the best illustrations of this who are known to any of us are Mrs. Julia Lake Kellersberger and her husband, Dr. Eugene Kellersberger, who have the responsibility of the American Leprosy Mission which is attempting to reach over 10,000,000 lepers with the gospel of Jesus Christ.[44]

Can we know "I am of the elect"? James Denney said, "Election has often been taught as if the one thing that could never be known about anybody was whether he was or was not elect." Paul's knowledge of their election came from what he had seen among them and what he had heard about them.[45]

Here are thirteen illustrations lifted out of one expository sermon. They represent quotations, personal experiences, historical references, the Bible, friendships, imagination, and the natural world. The creative imagination can supply illustrations. See Chapter 8 on imagination.

In concluding this chapter, then, we can say that the expository preacher should draw illustrations from all refined sources, beginning with the Bible. He can well avoid books of "canned" illustrations or any illustrations long worn out by overuse.

VII
Power Through
APPLICATION

A DISCOURSE WITHOUT APPLICATION would not be a sermon, but only a declamation—a monologue. "Where the application begins, there the sermon begins," said Spurgeon. We are not merely to speak before people but to them.

William Cleaver Wilkinson distinguished Phillips Brooks from Henry Ward Beecher on this basis: "For Mr. Brooks is not an orator such as Mr. Beecher was. He does not speak *to* people, *into* people, as Mr. Beecher did; rather he speaks *before* them, in their presence. He soliloquizes. There is almost a minimum of mutual relation between speaker and hearer. Undoubtedly the swift, urgent monolog is quickened, reinforced, by the consciousness of an audience present. That consciousness, of course, penetrates to the mind of the speaker. But it does not dominate the speaker's mind; it does not turn monolog into dialog; the speech is monolog still."[1]

Application means to put to use, to bring to bear upon, or to bring into contact with, as in the application of a poultice. It includes the idea of relevancy which is prominent in preaching theory today. Application brings the hearer under the claims of the gospel; it searches his heart and reins; it brings into divine encounter; it makes the listener say, "I am the man," or "He is speaking to me." Application "is the main thing to be done," says Broadus.

91

Truth is designed to be obeyed or practiced, not merely to furnish entertainment or information. Good application turns a sermon into a message. J. W. Etter said: ". . . and a preacher preaching a sermon without application would be like a physician giving to his patient a lecture on general health, and forgetting to write him a prescription."[2]

Therefore, the application may be considered the most important part of the sermon because it is the part that motivates the hearer to action. Without it, the sermon fails, because Biblical truth is meaningless unless it bears on life. It is better to make definite, searching application than to imply or hint at it.

How does one go about making application of sermonic truth? It may be done in several ways. The selection of a text and the framing of a title have application in mind. The phrasing of a sermon thesis should point in the direction of application. The explanatory part of an expository sermon often has elements of application in it. In making the truth plain, the bearing of that truth on conduct is almost certain to be evident. Sermon illustrations often help to make the relevancy of the truth manifest.

David R. Breed believed that application was also in the preacher. He wrote: "No preacher has any right to abdicate his function and refer his hearers only to a distant and disembodied divinity. The preacher must be the embodiment of the truth which he announces, and it must have with him a vital power. The mistake that some ministers make is that of thinking that truth contains its own force; but there is no force at all in mere truth. It is only when the truth takes hold on some man, and thus becomes incarnate, that it has influence and power. It is not true that 'truth is mighty and will prevail' if that truth be dissociated from a living and energetic personality. The application, therefore, is in the preacher. It has power because he is himself possessed by it."[3]

Audience analysis is necessary before the best application can be made. The preacher must know the nature and needs of his congregation in rather minute detail in order to offer the truth to them helpfully. We can always assume safely that a congregation has certain general spiritual needs—to repent, to believe, to pray, to forgive, to love, to serve, to grow, to study the Scriptures, to witness—because they are men in the flesh and not yet in heaven. True enough, but do they realize these needs? Are they trying to meet them? Or, have they become discouraged? Do they understand how to go about meeting these difficulties? What other more specific and more conscious needs do they now have?

In order to make sound and forceful application, truth must be lifted out of its local and temporary references and shown to be timeless and universal. There is something powerful about elemental, eternal truth. Such truth lies underneath the surface of all Biblical material. One of the major tasks of preaching is to find and lay bare these timeless truths in such a way that they will challenge and move listeners. These truths are essential to good sermon titles, theses, main points, and application. The normal mind has capacity to see and recognize at once the force of timeless truth. To apply such truth is relatively easy, for it almost applies itself. In order to grasp the significance of timeless truth, let us observe how some of the great expository preachers develop such truth here and there in their sermons.

Alexander Maclaren in his sermon, "Three Kinds of Praying," says:

Yes, God's delays are not delays, but are for our profit that we may always pray and not faint, and may keep alight the flame of sure hope that the Son of man cometh. . . .[4]

He who truly prays "sees no man any more," or if he does sees men only as subjects for intercession, not for contempt.[5]

In the judgment of heaven, which is the judgment of truth, sin forsaken is sin passed away.[6]

In his sermon on "Entering the Kingdom," Maclaren utters these eternal truths:

A great man's hangers-on are always more careful of his dignity than he is, for it increases their own importance.[7]

The infant's lowliness is not yet humility; for it is instinct rather than virtue. . . . On the other hand, clinging trust is the infant's life. It, too, is rudimentary and instinctive, but the impulse which makes the babe nestle in its mother's bosom may well stand for a picture of the conscious trust which the children of the kingdom must have.[8]

The entrance gate is very low, and if we hold our heads high, we shall not get through it. It must be on our hands and knees that we go into it.[9]

F. B. Meyer often developed these timeless, universal truths. From a few pages of his book, *Moses, the Servant of God*, we select these:

Nor will our lives ever be what they might until we realize that God has a plan for every hour in them; and that He waits to reveal that plan to the loving and obedient heart, making it known to us by one of the ten thousand ministries that lie around us.[10]

We are all too apt to run before we are sent, as Moses did in his first well-meant, but ill-timed, endeavours. We put our hands, at our own prompting, to a work that needs doing; we

94

ask God to help us, and we go on very well with the momentum of our own energy for at least a day. But on the morrow, when chiding and rebuke and difficulty arise, as they did to Moses, we are disappointed, and throw it all up; betaking ourselves to flight, finding our refuge in the solitudes of the desert.[11]

When God wants an implement for His service He does not choose the golden sceptre, but a shepherd's crook; the weakest and meanest thing He can find—a ram's horn, a cake of barley meal, an ox-goad, an earthen pitcher, a shepherd's sling. He employs a worm to thresh the mountains and makes the hills as chaff. A rod with God behind it is mightier than the vastest army.[12]

We only learn as we endeavour to obey. Light is given to us to know what next step we should take—just light enough and no more; a rim of light, hemmed in by darkness, falling as a faint circle on our path.[13]

And you will never get back into the warm, blessed circle of his manifested presence, where his face smiles and his voice speaks, till you have gone back to the place where you dropped the thread of obedience, and, taking it up where you left it, do what you know to be the word and will of God.[14]

G. Campbell Morgan was mighty in revealing timeless truth. Looking at his sermon on "Songs in Prison," based on Acts 16:25-26, we note the following:

At first we are amazed with the cheerfulness and heroism of these men, and then we find out that their singing was not abnormal but normal. It was not the result of a transient emotion. It was the expression of a constant experience of the soul.[15]

Their supreme consciousness was not that of the prison, or the stocks, or the pain, but of God. They were not callous or indifferent; pain was pain to them; confinement was confinement; loneliness was loneliness; but they realized how all these things were yet held in the grasp of the King of the perfect order, Whom they knew as their Lord and Master and, consequently, they sang praises.[16]

First, we learn that men who sing while they suffer are men who have learned the profound secret that suffering is the method by which joy is perfected.[17]

But again, men who sing in prison are men who cannot be imprisoned. . . . Fellowship with God is the franchise of eternity.[18]

And finally, men who sing when their work is stopped are men whose work is never stopped. . . . A man who can sing in prison is a man whose work is never done.[19]

That earthquake does not always come. We shall miss a great deal if we imagine that when we are in prison and sing, there will be an earthquake. Prison doors may not be opened at all. Thousands have been left in prison and died there, but they sang, and they sang through until they joined the new song on the other side. That earthquake does not matter.[20]

A few modern examples of timeless truth from Helmut Thielicke taken from his sermon on "The Parable of the Rich Man and Lazarus," Luke 16:19-31, may be appropriate:

It all depends upon one's identifying oneself with one of the five brothers and taking the right attitude toward the Word of God. This is the point of the story. Only as we start with this will the story be unlocked.[21]

In one way or another every one of us has this poor Lazarus

96

lying at our door, since every one, even the poorest of us, is in one way or another a rich man.[22]

For to be in hell simply means to be utterly separated from God. . . .[23]

It is the torment of the dead that they cannot warn the living, just as it is the torment of the mature that the erring young will not listen to them.[24]

Accordingly, there remains to us, the five brothers, nothing but "Moses and the prophets" and all that they have to say about this Jesus.[25]

The Bible deals with God's revelation in the past. The work of Christ in redemption was once-for-all in history. Preaching must speak with authority about these events and truths of the past, but the application of the truth must be brought into the present tense. ". . . now *is* the accepted time; behold, now *is* the day of salvation" (II Corinthians 6:2, KJV). Sin, Satan, the flesh, and the world are the same today as two thousand years ago. The work of God in Christ and the work of the Holy Spirit are as valid today as ever. The gospel has as much saving power now as in the first century. The needs of humanity in our affluent society are basically unchanged from Bible times.

The preacher's responsibility is to make the truths of the Bible contemporary and relevant. To do this, he will have to swing from the "they," "he," "she," and "it," to "you," the second person personal pronoun. "You" are the sinner who needs salvation; "you" are the church member who must experience redeeming grace; "you" are the youth whom Christ is calling; "you" are the one whom temptation has overcome and who must be cleansed. The preacher should not address God as "you" in his public

97

prayers, but he should frequently address his audience as "you."

As a magnifying glass brings the sun's rays to a burning focus upon a piece of grass or wood until it flames, so must the truth of the Scriptures be brought to a burning focus upon the lives of auditors until they respond to God's call. Jesus did not hesitate to do it. He said, "I tell you, No; but unless you repent you will all likewise perish" (Luke 13:3, rsv); and, "How can you believe, who receive glory from one another and do not seek the glory that comes from the only God? Do not think that I shall accuse you to the Father; it is Moses who accuses you, on whom you set your hope" (John 5:44-45, rsv).

Peter used the second person at Pentecost, ". . . Jesus of Nazareth, a man attested to you by God with mighty works and wonders and signs which God did through him in your midst, as you yourselves know—this Jesus, delivered up according to the definite plan and foreknowledge of God, you crucified and killed by the hands of lawless men" (Acts 2:22-23, rsv). When his hearers were cut to the heart, and cried, " 'Brethren, what shall we do?' . . . Peter said to them, 'Repent, and be baptized every one of you in the name of Jesus Christ for the forgiveness of your sins; and you shall receive the gift of the Holy Spirit' " (Acts 2:37-38, rsv).

Breed says that application includes recapitulation, illustration, inferences, and exhortation,[26] but it must go beyond that.

In his sermon on "Abel," Alexander Whyte bears down on our responsibility for our brother, in these words:

Where, then, is Abel thy brother? Answer that on the spot. Where hast thou hid him? Say on the spot, Lord, come with me and I will show Thee. Go back to Abel's grave. Go back continually in your past life. Go back to your school days. Go back to your college days. Go back to your first office, your first shop, your first workshop. Recall your first friend. Pass before your eyes the first young man, the first young woman, you were intimate with. Call up the long-mouldered corpse of your first affection, your first passion, your first love, your first lust. Give instances. Give names; and ask if God has another case like yours in all His Book. Face full in the face that monstrous folly; that word, that act, that makes you blush scarlet and turn in your seat to think of it. They are turning in their bed in hell at this moment for far less. . . . Why is introspection the only thing that you have no time for, and always push it into a corner? Is it because you are not your brother's keeper? Is it because you never struck a foul blow in the field? Is it because no grey head has ever gone down to a grave that your hands dug? Is it because no young man's faith, and no young woman's trust, and no unsuspecting friend's good name has ever been shaken, or deceived, or pulled down and murdered by you? Have your hands been always so washed in innocency? Are there no tears against you in God's bottle, and no names in His book?[27]

Whyte enforces the thought that when his first son was born, Enoch began to walk with God. In his sermon on "Enoch," his application is: "Fathers and mothers, young fathers and young mothers, fathers and mothers whose first child has just been born, and no more—seize your opportunity. Let not another day pass. Begin today. Begin tonight. It is late, if not yet too late, with the most of us; but it is not yet too late with you. Take Enoch for your father. Take him for your patron patriarch. Take him for your example. Follow him in his blessed footsteps in his family life."[28]

Broadus tells us that application should include practical suggestions concerning the best mode and means of performing the duty urged.[29] We can readily see how this is true. Many hearers do not understand how to go about practicing the good resolutions they make. They are dominated by carnal habits which are hard to break. Take the matter of prayer. People need to pray and they know it, but how to practice prayer effectively is what they have never been able to do. The preacher can suggest devotional books, prayer lists, prayer times, prayer places, prayer partners, prayer while driving, prayer retreats, and other useful practices.

In the matter of witnessing, almost all Christians would like to, but they do not know how to begin. They can be told about the value of keeping a Bible on the desk, how to circulate Christian literature and tracts, how to write witnessing letters, and how to bring Christ into ordinary conversations.

Christian families need help in practical procedures. Sermonic application can include ideas on family worship, family council, family purse, dividing the work load, taking vacations together, and worshiping together. Illustrations of how others are using unique and successful ways of practicing Christian ideals will enforce all such practical suggestions.

Modern psychological sermons have specialized on the "how to" emphasis, and many of them fail because they are more psychological than Scriptural. But that is no reason for the expository preacher to fail in the ways and means of application.

Under the title, "The Church's Attitude Toward Work," from the text, I Thessalonians 4:11 (KJV), " . . . study to be quiet, and to do your own business, and to work with your own hands. . . ," Harold J. Ockenga points up his application in these words:

100

Consistency of testimony is essential. Paul's word translated "honestly" is really seemingly or appropriately, but it has the meaning of honestly as well. It seems that we who are Christians working in an office for non-Christians must give a full labor value for the time for which we are paid. We cannot be chiselers, or clock-watchers, we cannot give fifty minutes for our sixty minutes pay, or seven hours work for our eight hours pay. To do so is to steal from those for whom we work. Some of the practices of our unions in America approximate that. When bricklayers are required to lay only two hundred bricks when they could lay twice that many in one day or when the machine that could lay several times that many is kept off the market, it is dishonest practice. This can be multiplied in many instances. On the other hand, when companies deliberately keep down the basic wages of employees, they encourage unions in such practices, or when companies refuse to share the profits which have been made by these employees, there is a certain degree of dishonesty involved, and Christians should give heed to these things. The Christian should be able to produce a better day's work, a better service, a better product than the man who is a non-Christian. This is the highest commendation of the Christian way of life.[30]

T. DeWitt Talmage had the right idea about the place of application in preaching. Preaching on "Jehu, the Swift Driver," he said: "Thus far my discourse may not have touched your case, and I consider that sermon a failure which does not strike every one somewhere. I have no desire to escape personal preaching. What is the use of going to church if not to be made better? I never feel satisfied when I sit in church unless the preacher strikes some of my sins and arouses me out of some of my stupidities."[31]

Preachers have differing sensitivities about pressing personalized application, and doubtless there is a difference in the abilities of ministers to do so; to do so with love, concern, tact and cogency is a capacity to be sought and cultivated.

The expository preacher, as well as all others, should not be satisfied except with positive response to his application. To do this requires the highest use of his imagination and persuasive skills. He should try to understand the art of motivation and use it according to Christian principles.

Human skills, techniques and capacities, no matter how excellent, are never enough in the field of preaching. There must be the backing and enduement of the Holy Spirit, in both the preparation and delivery of the sermon, if the sermon is to do its highest work. The Holy Spirit can work before, under, through, around, and after the words of the preacher strike the ears of the hearers. He can make suggestions, bring up memories, reveal needs, and motivate decisions that are vital, though they may never be known to the preacher. The preacher's privilege, then, is to seek the cooperation of the Holy Spirit in preaching.

VIII

Power Through
IMAGINATION

IMAGINATION IS ONE OF the most godlike capacities of man. It plays a significant role in all creative pursuits. The poet, the novelist, the dramatist, the musician, the painter, the sculptor, and the architect would be sadly handicapped without the use of imagination. The same thing is true in the commercial world. The inventor, the advertising man, the salesman, the radio broadcaster, the television producer, the business executive, the educator, the statesman, and the military leader must rely heavily on the power of imagination.

What about preaching? Yes, imagination plays an important role in preaching. Read what some of the homiletical authorities say.

Johann Michael Reu has written: "But an actor may select his words with the utmost care, and observe scrupulously all the laws of variety, euphony and rhythm; nevertheless, his oration will be beautiful only if at the same time imagination plays in it the role which belongs to it. Imagination rejoices in tropes and figures. She trails the ornamental epithet round the bare substantive as the gardener trails the ivy round the pillar. She loves to speed home her thought by climax and antithesis. She cultivates the figures of simile and metaphor in order to shed new light upon old truths, comparing spiritual with natural and natural with spiritual things."[1]

Daniel P. Kidder wrote: "Which, now, of the cognitive faculties conduces most to the gathering of new material for the preacher? Clearly the imagination; for while study enables us to perceive truth elaborated by others, memory to conserve it, and comparison and reflection to weigh it and determine its fitness, it is only imagination which penetrates the region of the new. . . . Imagination therefore must be regarded as the pioneer and leader of invention. . . . The truth is that neither artist nor poet needs so ready a use nor so perfect a control of the imagination as the public speaker."[2]

Andrew W. Blackwood has stated: "The biblical sermon is likely to be weak where it should be strong; that is, in appealing to the imagination. According to a mighty preacher, Horace Bushnell, the Gospel is 'a gift of God to the imagination.' "[3]

John A. Broadus wrote: "A preacher, without imagination, may be respected for his sound sense, may be loved for his homely goodness, but he will not move a congregation, he will not be a power in the community. . . . It is a matter on which preachers seldom bestow any thoughtful attention; and yet few things are so important to their real success, as the possession, the culture, the control, of imagination."[4]

Halford E. Luccock declared: "Using the image-making faculty in preaching is a means of helping people to see. And that is a primary purpose of sermons. . . . For the purpose of preaching is not to make people see reasons, but visions. . . ."[5]

In his Yale Lectures on preaching, R. W. Dale said: ". . . imagination is a most legitimate instrument of persuasion. It is an indispensable instrument. The minds of men are

104

sometimes so sluggish that we cannot get them to listen to us unless our case is stated with a warmth and a vigor which the imagination alone can supply."[6]

Walter Russell Bowie affirmed: "It is a 'sanctified imagination' that can lift a sermon up into the realm of poetry. . . . Too many men convey the great truths as thinly as though they were making a paper bag to put them in."[7]

What do we mean by imagination? It is the picture-making faculty of the mind. It is not the same as fancy, fiction, or daydreaming. Imagination is always under the control of reality. The fancy can soar into areas completely beyond the realm of human experience, or the possibility of human experience, and get out of touch with all reality —not so the imagination. Fancy can create the weird and impossible—ghosts, goblins, brownies, fairies, space ships from other planets—but imagination stays with the hard, concrete facts of known existence. Dreams and daydreaming combine the real with the fantastic and lift the individual into a grotesque world of unreality. Imagination can combine the real into new combinations, and can pierce through the visible and tangible to lay bare the underlying principles of eternal truth. Imagination can see what might have been, what can now be, and what might yet be, with the same vividness as it sees what is.

The dictionary definition of imagination is this: "a) the act or power of forming mental images of what is not actually present. b) the act or power of creating mental images of what has never been actually experienced, or of creating new images or ideas by combining previous experiences; creative power.

"*Imagination* is often regarded as the more seriously and deeply creative faculty, which perceives the basic resemblances between things, as distinguished from *fancy*, the

105

lighter and more decorative faculty, which perceives superficial resemblances."[8]

The imagination may be abused and wrongly used. Before the Flood, "every imagination of the thoughts of his [man's] heart was only evil continually" (Genesis 6:5, KJV). The Biblical reason for the darkness and lostness of the heathen world, according to Paul in Romans 1:21 (KJV), is that, ". . . when they knew God, they glorified him not as God, neither were thankful; but became vain in their imaginations, and their foolish heart was darkened." But we are thinking about the valid use of imagination in expository preaching. Perhaps we can distinguish four uses of this splendid faculty.

In dealing with the historical or narrative material of the Bible, the imagination can fill in the details as they might well have happened. The preacher should avoid bringing twentieth-century details into Biblical scenes; that would be anachronism. But he can use considerable liberty in painting a scene against its own proper background.

Alexander Maclaren was quite restrained in the use of his imagination but he does light up the Biblical events here and there with flashes of imagination. In his sermon on Zacchaeus, "Melted By Kindness," we note these uses of imagination:

We know how the rich taxgatherer, pocketing his dignity, and unable to see over the heads of the crowd, scrambled up into the branches of the sycamore tree that overhung the road; and there was found by the eye of love, and surprised by the words of kindness, which melted him down, and made a new man of him on the spot.[9]

It would be a sight to bring jeers and grins on the faces of the crowd to see the rich man of the custom-house sitting up

106

amongst the leaves. But he did not mind about that if he got a good look at the Rabbi when He passed.[10]

When the little procession stopped under the sycamore tree, Zacchaeus would begin to feel uncomfortable. He may have had experience in past times of the way in which the great doctors of orthodoxy were in the habit of treating a publican, and may have begun to be afraid that this new one was going to be like all the rest, and elicit some kind of mob demonstration against him. The crowd would be waiting with intense curiosity to see what would pass between the Rabbi and the revenue collector. . . . Perhaps it was the first time since he had been a child at his mother's knees that he had heard his name pronounced in tones of kindness.[11]

People had frowned on Zacchaeus, and it made him bitter. They had execrated and persecuted him; and his only response was setting his teeth more firmly and turning the screw a little tighter when he had the chance.[12]

G. Campbell Morgan also was modest in his imaginative material, but he did bring his imagination into play frequently. From his sermon on Acts 16:25-26, "Songs in Prison," we select these passages: "Their backs were bruised and bleeding and unwashed. They were cast into the inner prison, some inner chamber or dungeon from which light was excluded and probably almost all air was shut out. The final barbarity was that their feet were made fast in the stocks."[13]

A second use is the creative one. Morgan so used it but he was always true to reality. Here is an example from the same sermon: "Your sorrow shall be turned into joy. . . . Look back over the years. There they are, travel-worn years; much of light is upon them, but much of darkness also; many days of triumph, marching with the band playing and the flags flying, and many days of disaster and defeat. Already you know that the greatest things of life have come, not out of the sunlit days, but out of the darkened hours."[14]

Frequently the preacher will be at a loss to find a fitting illustration for a particular point. None of his books or files yield one that suits. Let him see if he can imagine an illustration. He should introduce it with such words as: "Let us suppose . . .," "Imagine that . . .," "Can you conceive . . . ?" A good imaginary illustration can be more closely fitted to the material that it illustrates than any other because it is invented exactly for that purpose. Here are two imaginary illustrations that the author has used.

The first one illustrates justification by faith:

Suppose you are one thousand dollars in debt to the largest department store in this city. You have no money to pay, and you have no credit to borrow any money. The store keeps sending you bills, and you keep hoping that you will find a way to get the money to pay, but you do not. They threaten to sue, but you cannot pay. You get a letter from the store. You say, "Another bill! What shall I do? Maybe I will have to go to jail over this bill." And you open the letter fearfully. You read: "Dear customer: We are glad to notify you that a friend of yours, who does not wish his name known, has come in and paid your bill in full. More than that, he has deposited another thousand dollars with us to your credit. Now, instead of you owing us one thousand dollars we owe you one thousand dollars. Please come in and use your credit."

You are amazed. You can say one of three things: 1) "That must be a mistake. I have no friend who thinks that much of me. I will go down and tell the store they have the accounts confused." That would be unbelief. 2) "I appreciate that friend's desire to help, but I cannot allow it. I make my own way, and no one is going to pay my bills but myself." That would be re-

108

jection. 3) "Thank God, for such a friend! Come on, wife, let's go down to the store and use our credit." That would be faith. Justification pays your debt to God for all your sins. It wipes the slate clean in remission of your sins, but it does more. It puts the righteousness of Christ down to your credit. You not only are out of debt, but you have as much credit standing as Christ can give you.

You can be unbelieving, rejecting, or accepting.

This illustration is purely imaginary but the writer has had good response to it.

The second illustration is of salvation by grace through faith apart from works of any kind:

Two men in a certain town were born the same day and have lived there all their lives. One has ever gone the way of morality, good works and uprightness, but the other has always gone the way of sin, Satan, the flesh and the world. From their 50th birthdays onward they have annually had a little birthday dinner party together. The moral man has always tried to turn the sinner from his wickedness but with no success.

On the day they are both eighty years old, they meet for the usual birthday dinner. On the way back to their homes they stop together to listen to a Salvation Army street meeting. Neither man up to this point has ever made a profession of faith in Christ. The Salvation group preaches salvation by grace through faith apart from good works, and presses the invitation. The wicked eighty-year-old, a drunkard, a liar, a swearer, a scoundrel, receives Christ and confesses him publicly before men. The other eighty-year-old rests in his good works and scoffs at emotional religion. They cross the street together and are hit by a speeding, drunken driver and both killed instantly. Which one went to heaven? If you say the good moral man, you are making salvation to be by character and good works. If you say the poor old sinner, the moral failure, you are making salvation to be by grace through faith apart from works, and you are right.

A third function depicts the future. It may forsee the blackness of the lost sinner's life as he goes on without Christ and God, or it may describe the carnal Christian's coming days when his works pass through the fire and are all burned.

Futuristic imagination also deals with the events of the last times, the second coming of Christ, the judgment scenes, the glories of heaven and the terrors of hell. Care must be taken not to go beyond what is written, or what is true to the character of God and the total of Biblical revelation.

G. Campbell Morgan, in his sermon, "Songs in Prison," makes this reference to the future: ". . . men who sing at midnight are citizens of that city of which it is said that they need no light of the sun or moon, for the Lord and the Lamb are the light of it . . . Abraham lived in it though he never saw it; he walked its streets though it was never built; he held communion with its inhabitants though he never reached it. Paul and Silas, where are you living just now? In Philippi? No, in the City of God!"[15]

Morgan takes another imaginative peep into the future on the human level in this quotation from the same sermon: "The singing of a prisoner is a message to prisoners and they will listen. I cannot go any further. I do not know what happened to those prisoners afterwards. If you will allow the speculation, I believe that some of them were brought to Jesus Christ as the result of that singing. Cancel that if you do not agree."[16]

The fourth possibility is the use of imagination in entering into the experiences of others and seeing life through their eyes. It creates sympathy and understanding. D. L. Moody approaches sympathetic imagination when he describes Barabbas in his cell awaiting execution the next day: "Maybe they let his mother come to see him

110

once more before dark. Perhaps he had a wife and children, and they came to see him for the last time. He could not sleep at all that night. He could hear somebody hammering in the prison yard and knew they must be making the cross. He would start up every now and then, thinking that he heard the footsteps of officers coming for him.

"At last the light of the morning looks in through the bars of the prison.

" 'Today—this very day—they will open that door and lead me away to be crucified!'

"Pretty soon he hears them coming. No mistake this time. They are unbarring the iron door. He hears them turning the key in the rusty lock. Then the door swings open. There are the soldiers.

"Goodbye to life and hope! Death—horrible death—now! And after death—what will there be then?

"The officer of the guard speaks to him: 'Barabbas, you are free.' "[17]

T. DeWitt Talmage was outstanding in the use of his imagination. The following from his sermon on "Isaac Rescued" is a sample: "So Isaac's arms are fastened, his feet are tied. The old man rallying all his strength, lifts him up on a pile of wood. Fastening a thong on one side of the altar he makes it span the body of Isaac, and fastens the thong at the other side of the altar, and another thong, and another thong. There is the lamp flickering in the wind, ready to be put under the brushwood of the altar. There is the knife, sharp and keen. Abraham—struggling with his mortal feelings on the one side, and the commands of God on the other—takes that knife, rubs the flat of it on the palm of his hand, cries to God for help, comes up to the side of the altar, puts a parting kiss on the brow of the boy, then takes a message from him for mother and home, and then, lifting the glittering weapon for the plunge of

111

the death stroke—his muscles knitting for the work—the hand begins to descend. It falls! Not on the heart of Isaac, but on the arm of God, who arrests the stroke, making the wilderness quake with the cry: 'Abraham! Abraham! lay not thy hand upon the lad, nor do him any harm.' "[18]

This example of imagination is largely historical but it also enables the listeners to enter into the experience of Abraham sympathetically.

We have already shown something of Alexander Whyte's use of imagination. Let us follow him again. Speaking about the resurrection of Lazarus, he imagines the experience of Lazarus being called back from death to life: "And thus it was that scarcely had Lazarus sat down in his Father's house: he had not got his harp of gold well into hand: he had not got the Hallelujah that they were preparing against the Ascension of their Lord well into his mouth, when the angel Gabriel came up to where he sat, all rapture through and through, and said to him: 'Hail, Lazarus, highly honored among the glorified from among men. Thy Master calls up for thee. He has some service for thee still to do for Him on earth.' And the sound of many waters fell silent for a season as they saw one of the most shining of their number rise up, and lay aside his glory, and hang his harp on the wall, and pass out of their sight, and descend to where their heavenly Prince still tarries with His work unfinished. And Lazarus' soul descended straightway into that grave, where for four days his former body had lain dead, and towards which our Lord was now on His way."[19]

Or, let us stand with the sinners Whyte weighs in the balances in his sermon on Belshazzar: "Belshazzar was weighed with weights of his own, that no man before nor since has ever been weighed with but Belshazzar himself. And you will be weighed, you are being weighed at this

112

moment, with your own proper weights also. God Almighty has a special pair of balances beside Him, waiting and filling up till your life also is numbered and finished. Look up, sinner, at the awful instrument. Forecast the awful scene. All that God has done for you in your birth, in your godly upbringing, in your means of grace, in providences, and in all privileges, in divine calls to a better life; all such warnings, and all such instructions are collecting into one scale, and your soul—your naked and shivering soul—into the other scale with the whole universe looking on. Well may your knees knock! Well may your thoughts trouble you."[20]

This quotation illustrates how to gear the power of imagination to the creation of new material and to the use of it in application.

An example of the futuristic use of imagination comes from Clarence E. Macartney, a Bible preacher though not regularly an expository preacher. In his sermon on "Isaiah —the Man Who Saw Christ's Glory" he tells us that one of the glories of heaven will be listening to the great heroes of the Bible preach from day to day: Moses, Jeremiah, John the Baptist, Peter, John and Paul. But when the seventh day comes: "I imagine the preacher for the day by universal consent will be Isaiah; and we shall see these great preachers I have named, and all the prophets and apostles . . . sitting at the feet of Isaiah and listening to him. . . ."[21]

What a way to arouse interest in Isaiah—the man and the book!

Both the introduction and the conclusion are vital parts of the sermon. Unless the introduction elicits the interest of the hearers and leads them to the theme and thesis of the sermon, the preacher has lost part of his opportunity. Therefore, an introduction should be vitally related to the body of the sermon, interesting, brief, clear, simple, and modest. The worst way to begin is to start talking about the text or its backgrounds in a matter-of-fact way. A better beginning is an illustration, a quotation, an observation, or a striking statement. Imagination can play an important part in creating the introduction. The preacher can say to himself, "If I were to hear this sermon, what introduction would I like?" "Rather than use the usual type of introduction, could I use something imaginary and suppositional with more striking effect?" If we give imagination a chance it will often create exactly the right idea.

The expository preacher should keep his introduction short because he has so much material to present in the main body of the sermon. However, he cannot make it too short, or leave it half-prepared. The right procedure is to prepare all the rest of the sermon first. Then his introduction can be exactly tailored to that particular sermon.

Joseph Parker was noted for his active imagination. He used it to create the introduction to his sermon on Matthew 24:1-41, "The Exciting Element in Christ's Ministry," in these words: "Imagine a river very broad and deep, rolling quietly and rhythmically for long miles, not a bubble upon the surface, no noise, no tumult, a great, deep, strong, noble stream of water, and imagine that stream suddenly coming to a terrific precipice. What a cataract, what a roar and rush and tumult, what rainbows made by the sun, what snowy veils and screens, what infinite wizardry of shape and sound and suggestion! It does not look like the same water. Nothing is so accommodating as water; it will do anything, it will allow itself to be broken up into little drops that shall sparkle like diamonds in the shining sun, and gather itself into great masses and carry navies as if they were straws driven by the wind. It will run through gardens, it will come into houses dripping and dropping just to suit the capacity of your little cup; it will gather

114

itself into infinite blackness in the heavens, and fall in daily baptism upon the thirsty earth. There is nothing so genial, yet so terrible, as water—unless indeed, it be its mate and contrast, fire. It is even so with these speeches of Christ."[22]

This introduction may be somewhat elaborate and over-drawn but it is captivating and individualistic.

In a sermon on "The Gift of the Gospel," Romans 1:14-18, the writer introduces it in words somewhat like these: "Suppose you had the opportunity to do something great, good and breath-taking for your world, what would you choose to do? Would it be to wipe out crime at a single stroke? Or, to do away with ignorance? Or, to eliminate poverty all over the world in one day? Or, to banish war forever and bring in universal peace? Any of these would be towering contributions and would insure your fame through all coming history. But if you asked Paul, the writer of our text, this question, he would have but one answer: 'I choose to give the world the gospel of Christ.'"

Imagination developed this introduction. It prepares the audience to consider why the gift of the gospel is so important.

Similarly the conclusion should be well prepared. If the introduction is like the porch to a house, the conclusion is like the roof. It too must be brief, clear, appropriate, vitally related to the discussion it follows, interesting, and persuasive. Recapitulation is usually appropriate in the conclusion but it is not enough. There should be the focusing of truth upon the hearer, the suggestion of ways and means of practicing it, and the appeal for action. All of this must be done in a short time or the sermon becomes too long. Imagination can help formulate the conclusion. If the preacher lets his imagination play over the sermon it can suggest an appropriate and compelling close. He is seeking not just any conclusion, but the very best one.

Notice Joseph Parker's use of imagination in the con-

clusion of his sermon on Matthew 27:20-54, "The Crucifixion," when he says: "O thou great hell, take the victory.
Spirit of evil, damned from all eternity, mount the central
cross and mock the dead as thou hast mocked the living!
The night is dark enough—no such night ever settled upon
the earth before. Will the light ever come again—is the
sun clean gone forever—will the blue sky ever more kiss
the green earth? All the birds are dead, their music is
choked; the angels have fled away and the morning stars
have dropped their sweet hymn. This is chaos with an
added darkness. What is happening?

"May be God and Christ are communing in the secret
places away beyond the mountains of night—may be that
this *murder* will become the world's *Sacrifice*—may be
that out of this blasphemy will come a Gospel for every
creature. It cannot end where it is—*that* cannot be the end
of all! What will come next? We must wait."[23]

But suppose you say, "I have no imagination"? We admit
that some people display very little imagination; they live
humdrum, matter-of-fact lives. But the truth is that every
person has imagination. All little children live in the world
of imagination and fancy. They are sometimes unable to
distinguish the real from the imaginary and fanciful. The
process of modern education tends to develop the reasoning powers but neglects the imagination. But schools of
art, music, drama, and writing must pay attention to culti-
vating the imagination.

We can cultivate imagination by reading and meditating
upon the Bible. It is a Book of colorful, poetic, and dramatic material. By ministering to others and sympathetically entering into their problems and needs, the imagination becomes active in seeking to meet their needs. By
reading poetry, drama, fiction, biography, and noting the
metaphors, similes, comparisons, analogies, allegories, we

116

will develop the imaginative faculty. When we listen to good music and let it carry us away into the realms of harmony and meditation, we are ministering to the imagination. By conscious effort in sermonizing, we can add touches of imaginative material, and often we can recast the Biblical scenes in realistic but imaginary backgrounds.

IX

Power Through
PREPARATION

By NOW YOU MAY be feeling that expository preaching requires too much preparation time to be seriously and regularly undertaken. Homiletical authorities commonly agree that the expository is the hardest type of preaching and that it usually requires more time in preparation. We do not minimize these facts. However, we do hope to show that it is possible to save time without stinting preparation.

Ministers today live under the pressure of many demands upon their time. This has been called the maceration of the minister. Our survey questionnaire revealed that 153 out of 223 pastors considered lack of sufficient preparation time their chief problem. This figure was nearly forty per cent higher than that reported for their second problem, that of finding good illustrations.

Pastors have one big advantage over most other callings —they can plan their own time schedules. This allows them to give priority to the duties they think most important. Certainly preaching stands first in the minds of most ministers and parishioners, in the order of pastoral duties. No pastor should expect to prepare for it with tag ends of time. Any type of preaching should require a sizable bulk of time. Wilbur M. Smith has written: "I know of no quick road to worth-while preaching. It is hard work,

119

but wonderfully rewarding. We are living in a day of superficial, inconsequential, unmoving preaching."[1]

Let us make a few suggestions regarding the conservation of time for expository preaching.

First, the pastor should block out and set aside certain periods of time for sermon preparation and general study. Four hours a day on four mornings of the week are little enough. If these periods are broken into, then he shall have to try to make up the time at other points during the day. Periods of study shorter than two or three hours are not satisfactory. It takes time to get the books and equipment into place and to warm up the mental machinery, but periods longer than three or four hours may cause weariness and lessening of accomplishment.

Second, planning one's sermons for several weeks or months ahead can save time. If the expository preacher plans to preach through a book of the Bible, or a sermon series of five to ten sermons, he has a real advantage. While preparing one sermon, the pastor finds material appropriate for future sermons and drops it into the proper file envelope.

Third, beginning early in the week on the sermon or sermons for the following Sunday puts the mind on the alert to capture ideas and illustrations throughout the week.

Fourth, carrying a notebook in the pocket and a commentary in the automobile may help in recording good ideas during spare minutes.

Fifth, a time of regular personal Bible study will not only furnish spiritual strength to the soul, but will turn up Biblical illustrations and thoughts for current sermons. The preacher must learn to live by the same Word he preaches to his people.

Sixth, forming the habit of expository preaching will

120

eventually save time. The preacher forms homiletical habits and builds up a background of Biblical knowledge that makes him more effective. Gradually the thrill and joy of expository sermon preparation will be so great that the preacher will regret turning to other duties. William G. Coltman told the writer that he prepared two expository sermons every week whether he preached them or not. Even when he knew he was to have a guest preacher in the pulpit, he prepared his two expository sermons for that Sunday just the same. He felt he could not afford to break his homiletical habits or to miss the pleasure of preparing to preach the Word.

Seventh, keep right with God. Expository preaching is no practice for a backsliding preacher. The strength and power of the Word simply will not distill into the mind and heart of the man living in disobedience. He will be like Samson with his locks of hair shorn, or like David trying to use Saul's armor.

Let us emphasize this truth regarding time spent in sermon preparation: sermons are poor or good, other things being equal, in proportion to the time spent in preparing them. Paul S. Rees asserted that he spent approximately twenty-five hours out of each week on direct and intensive preparation for the two Sunday sermons. When Walter A. Maier was preaching regularly on the "Lutheran Hour," he said he spent one hour in preparation for every minute he preached. H. E. Fosdick made the same claim for his preparation of his sermons at Riverside Church in New York. If homiletical geniuses require so much preparation time, can average preachers afford to skimp?

We have already emphasized the necessity for good source material for expository preaching. Many pastors have poor libraries for this purpose. The preacher needs half a dozen good commentaries on any passage he undertakes to expound. If he can use the original languages, he can get along on fewer. The use of lexicons and concordances was discussed in the chapter on explanation. How can a pastor obtain the books he needs?

It is better to have a few good ones and use them than to have many ordinary books of limited value. If a man concentrates his expository preaching on one Bible book for a series of weeks, perhaps he can buy two or three new exegetical commentaries on that one book. If he cannot afford to buy, maybe he can borrow a few helpful books from fellow pastors. Some of the local libraries may be able to help him. A pastor's wife can often help him obtain wanted books by guiding parishioners to certain volumes for his birthday, anniversary or Christmas. Better to have books than neckties or golf shoes. Now and then a pastor's widow will sell quite reasonably, or even give away her husband's library. The preacher might watch for any such bonanza. Once in a while people of the parish will have good books which they have inherited or bought, but are no longer using; if the pastor shows an interest in such books, they may give them to him, or at least lend them. Another workable plan is to establish a new book fund from funeral fees, wedding fees, and honoraria from extra speaking engagements.

Expensive sets are seldom worth the price. Better buy individual commentaries of known worth.

Any passage of Scripture should be thoroughly investigated as suggested in the chapter on explanation. This investigation should proceed carefully and in a somewhat leisurely fashion in order to note all angles and bits of information. Many a passage that seems dull and dry on casual reading will come alive as thoughtful investigation proceeds. The careful expositor will be as thorough as he possibly can in the investigative process. He will not hesitate to abandon traditional interpretations if evidence justifies. But he will not buy new ideas just because they are new. While he will respect consensus and will not discard it quickly, he will never regard it as sacred. He will take long, hard looks at what the Bible says and what the commentators say it means. He will pay no premium for the new and startling, but he will not reject it if evidence supports it.

Investigation may include talks with fellow pastors about the interpretation of certain passages, or even telephone calls to Biblical authorities.

The Scriptures yield extra bonuses to the process of meditation. Moses said, ". . . you shall meditate on it day and night . . ." (Joshua 1:8, RSV). And the Psalmist wrote, ". . . his delight is in the law of the Lord, and on his law he meditates day and night" (Psalms 1:2, RSV). During His Satanic temptations in the wilderness, Jesus declared, "It is written, 'Man shall not live by bread alone, but by every word that proceeds from the mouth of God'" (Matthew 4:4, RSV). In meditation, the preacher does relaxed thinking about his expository passage. He mulls or broods over it as he walks, drives, or sits alone. He is half in prayer and half in reflective thought. He is turning the passage over and over in his mind, asking it questions and comparing various interpretations. After getting into bed at night, he may still continue meditating about his text. He is not worrying or doubting, but is beholding it in wonder, inquiry and contemplation. He thanks God for the privilege of thinking His thoughts after Him. Thus as he drops off to sleep his unconscious mind takes over and deals with the passage. In the morning he may awake with new ideas and approaches.

Meditation can never be a hurried and pressured process. It takes time, but it can be spare time. It is a refreshing exercise for the mind and the soul of the preacher. While it goes on, the Scripture passage is soaking in and taking hold of the preacher's spiritual outlook. The more meditation the text receives, the better the ensuing sermon will be.

As he investigates and meditates, the pastor will be making notes. He will not try to keep them in any particular order but will jot ideas down as they occur. For this purpose, he needs note pads always at hand—in his pocket and his car. He will not mind if he writes the same ideas down several times. His notes will include not only ideas, questions, comments, applications, illustrations, but hints for an outline as well. Again, he should not have to hurry in his note-making.

After a time he will assemble all his notes and go through them for the purpose of making his final outline, or at least his working outline. Once his outline has been completed, he will jot into it the material for expanding it—explanations, arguments, illustrations, applications. This is not writing out the sermon in full but merely getting all his material in order.

A sermon must take the form of specific words either during preparation or delivery, or both. A sermon cannot exist merely as detached ideas, or as an outline. Many good men stop short of completing their sermon preparation. They preach from skeletons or briefs of sermons. They have never pushed the process on to the point of putting every idea into particular words. They depend on the inspiration of the occasion and their own powers of extemporizing to give them the exact words in delivery. Preachers who do this will always be inexact, repetitious, and abstract. Their style will be rough, wretched and ragged.

A sermon must be verbalized in order to be communicated. The better one verbalizes the sermon in his study, the better the pulpit delivery will be. This does not necessarily mean that the whole sermon must be written in full, though most of the greatest preachers do write out their sermons completely. W. E. Sangster wrote: "It is the man who has never written his sermons out, and never intends to, who is almost certainly doomed to unconscious repetition and mediocrity. Without being aware of it, he repeats himself in ideas, in illustrations and phrasing."[2]

In an article in *Look* magazine some months ago, Ralph W. Sockman described his method of verbalizing as follows: "I do it the hard way, all hunched over, writing the sermon in longhand, with books opened up all over my desk. By the end of the afternoon, I may have 25 pages."[3]

Other pastors feel that writing sermons takes too much time and work. They hate the mechanical slavery of writing, and believe that they lose their inspiration and fire while writing. If they can verbalize as completely some other way, none can object to the omission of writing. There are three or four other ways to verbalize the sermon apart from writing it.

A very practical one is to preach the sermon from notes into a tape recorder. This gets the sermon down exactly as the preacher has verbalized it. As he listens to the recording, the preacher should make notes: of his mistakes, of new ideas that flash upon him, of parts of the message he wishes to revise. With these corrections and additions indicated in his notes, the preacher should preach it again to his recorder. It would be better to let an interval of time elapse before recording it the second time. Another hearing, revision and playback would be desirable. On Sunday morning before going to his church, the preacher should listen to the second or third recording so as to refresh his mind with the sermon.

The disadvantage of the recording method is that one

never gets any sermon in writing so he can examine it minutely. He may have a library of taped sermons but he has nothing to publish in magazines or books. The advantage is that he hears himself as he actually is. He will probably feel quite humble and be anxious to improve.

A better method, but one not available to many pastors, is to dictate the sermon to a secretary and have her type it in full. Then the preacher can go over his manuscript carefully to make the necessary revisions and corrections. A typing of the revised manuscript should put the sermon into proper shape for absorbing or memorizing. This method has been used by such preachers as Clovis G. Chappell, Clarence E. Macartney, and Harold J. Ockenga. But this method may not be as easy as it sounds. To do it, a preacher must be a very clear and fluent thinker, or he must verbalize his sermon to himself enough times so that he can dictate it straight through without fumbling and stumbling.

Many tape recorders are equipped with transcribing devices. With such a machine, the pastor can take his time in his study for recording and correcting his message, then the secretary can take her time transcribing it from the tape. In either or both of these cases, we believe the preacher makes a mistake if he utterly flees the writing experience. He needs it in order to perfect his thinking, his fluency, and his style. If he does not write sermons, let him write articles, essays and books for publication. He will be a better preacher if he does.

Then there is the rehearsal method of verbalizing, or talking it out loud. James Gordon Gilkey first writes the sermon then rehearses it several times. His words are: "So after my sermon has been completed as a piece of written work it must be rehearsed as a piece of public address. I always preach a sermon several times to the furniture in

126

my study before attempting to preach it to the people in my church. Only then can the sermon be delivered without notes and with the proper rhythm, movement and climax."[4]

Others follow the method of Gerald Kennedy—verbalizing from notes rather than full manuscript. He has said: "The next morning (Thursday) I take the outline and scratchy notes into a room where I can talk it out loud. This seems to me important, because preaching is not only bringing thoughts to people, it is also finding words to make the thoughts march. Sometimes a preacher gives the impression of having the thoughts in order, but the way of presenting them has an unfinished, almost rough manner. At any rate, it may be a good thing to try speaking the sermon out loud if its effectiveness is not quite up to par . . . I speak it through again Friday morning, again Saturday morning, and then parts of it early Sunday morning. By that time I am ready to preach without any notes. . . . Each time the sermon is gone through, the preacher becomes a little more free from his paper, partly because the material begins to flow from one point to another."[5]

Other men believe that they can achieve full verbalization without any writing at all. They simply rehearse the sermon to themselves and speak either extemporaneously or from brief notes. Joseph Parker followed this method in his later life. F. R. Webber says of him: "During his early ministry he wrote his sermons, but in later life he learned to speak extemporaneously, with marvellous precision and force. He selected a text early in the week, then walked Hampstead Heath, concentrating his thoughts upon his text. . . . He paid little attention to actual words. He carried with him to the pulpit his text, written with a lead pencil on a small piece of paper, and a few lines suggesting the main thoughts in their orderly sequence. The presence of his great congregation of 3,000 or more people gave him

127

the required fire, and he expressed himself in language whose force and beauty any preacher might envy."[6]

Parker's method worked for him, but would it for you?

Prayer and verbalizing go together. The idea is to pray through the sermon either on one's knees or by walking up and down in the study. Whether the sermon has been fully written, dictated, recorded, or merely compiled in notes, the practice of praying over it sentence by sentence and paragraph by paragraph is an excellent one. Billy Sunday said that no matter how often he preached a sermon, he always soaked it in prayer before each presentation. The Holy Spirit can use this prayer-saturation period to inspire additions or deletions in what has been prepared.

There would seem to be no one best way to achieve the verbalizing stage of sermon preparation. Each preacher will have to find those methods that work best for him. If he can write it out in full, this should be his aim. If he preaches twice on Sunday, perhaps he need write out only one sermon completely. But the verbalizing must not be omitted. It is at his own peril that the preacher neglects this process.

When the sermon has been fully prepared, what shall the preacher take into the pulpit? A full manuscript? Full notes? Brief notes? An outline? A few catch words? Or, nothing at all? Again, a man must experiment and find out for himself what is best. J. H. Jowett preached from a full manuscript, but had his sermon so fully absorbed, and handled his manuscript so skillfully, that very few people realized he used one. Many great preachers have been manuscript preachers.

But something about preaching from a manuscript does not seem to be consistent with prophetic and apostolic practice. Listeners generally do not care for manuscript preaching. They rightly feel that a sermon should be a message from God spoken directly from preacher to people. Therefore, extemporaneous delivery without manuscript or notes of any kind would be the popular preference. The pastor should cultivate this ability, and most men can do it if they really try. The biggest requirement for preaching without notes is to have a logical, coherent outline that can easily be memorized. If the sermon has been carefully put together, it will all hang to the outline. When the outline consists of three or four simple but progressive main points, stemming out of a thesis through a key word, preaching without notes is not so difficult. Clarence E. Macartney preached entirely without notes, and today so does Harold J. Ockenga. This is the ideal way.

However, the majority of preachers prefer to have some kind of notes. Admittedly notes do relieve pulpit pressure and aid the memory to recall the whole sermon. The trouble is that notes may grow too complex and lengthy. In that case, they are almost as objectionable as a full manuscript. If one is to use notes, he should reduce them to one side of one page, so that there is no turning of pages.

The writer has found that all the notes necessary can be typed on one side of a 4" x 6" file card; the card is then fastened into one's Bible, opposite the passage used for a text. Two square, non-tearing paper clips at the top and two on the side hold the note card firmly in place, so that it cannot possibly fall out or blow away, and this type of paper clip does not tear or mar the pages in a Bible. For best results, one should capitalize, indent, underline, and use different colors. Here is a sample based on our familiar passage, Luke 18:1-8.

Praying Always—Luke 18:1-8

All of us believe in prayer, but most of us fail in it. This parable teaches us to pray at all times, or on all occasions, and not to forget or faint or give up.

Our passage reveals four reasons for praying always.

I. Our Lord urged it, v. 1
  1. This is reason enough for true believers.
  2. Jesus Himself practiced it.
  3. It can be done if we try.
II. Life's emergencies require it, vv.2-5
  1. This widow faced a real crisis.
  2. She prayed always to a wicked judge.
  3. Emergencies requiring prayer come to us, to our loved ones, to friends.
III. God's mercies encourage it, vv.6-8
  1. Our God is the opposite of the wicked judge. He hears their cries.
  2. He is just and long-suffering.
IV. Son of man's return seeks it, v.8
  1. When Christ returns He will seek the faith that prays always.
  2. He will render full and speedy justice.
  3. Will He find "the faith" in you?
Conclusion: Make prayer the unbroken habit and major force in your life. When we faint instead of praying, prayer becomes a farce instead of a force.

With his sermon fully prepared, and his pulpit notes fixed in the proper place, the minister can now relax. All he will need to do now is to give his sermon a quick review and commit himself to God in prayer before he goes into the pulpit. He can rest well on Saturday night. He should see that he gets his full quota of sleep so that he will be at his physical, mental and spiritual best at the time of sermon delivery. He can now have a fair measure of assurance that he has done his best in sermon preparation and can expect God to back his human best with the

130

enduement of the Holy Spirit. Power through adequate preparation will insure power in communicating his sermon.

Is the expository sermon harder to communicate than the topical or textual? At first thought, it would seem to be; it is more confined in what it is and what it can do. But, on second thought, the expository discourse may be easier to communicate than other types of sermons. It deals with Biblical material of vital interest to church attenders, and therefore enlists the sympathies of the listeners with the preacher. It bestows an authority upon both messenger and message that requires a hearing and a response.

The preacher, or his congregation, or both, may hinder the process of communication. The preacher may not be aware that such a problem exists; he may lead an ivory-tower existence out of touch with the problems and needs of his people; he may speak in theological, philosophical, or scholastic terminology which has little meaning to his congregation; he may live such a shallow spiritual life that he has no vital message; he may so expend his time and energies on churchly duties that he does not have time enough to prepare challenging sermons; his voice, gestures and pulpit delivery may be so poor that they hinder rather than help him.

The congregation may prevent communication by lack of spiritual growth, by preoccupation with the cares and pleasures of life, by involvement in worldly practices out of line with Biblical living, by suspicions and jealousies of one another, by secularization, and by hardening of heart. Then, too, the acoustics of the building may be poor, the seating arrangements awkward, the ventilation and lighting insufficient, and outside noises and sights too distracting. Any or all these can hinder communication.

X
Power Through
COMMUNICATION

THE SUPREME TEST OF a sermon is whether or not it communicates. If it fails here, all else is in vain. Several terms have been used to describe the preacher's pulpit action. An old one is "to preach" the sermon; a newer one is "to deliver" the sermon, and a still newer one is "to present" the message. All of these focus attention upon the preacher and the sermon almost to the exclusion of the audience. They imply that the preacher's responsibility ends with speaking the message from the pulpit. The audience may do whatever it pleases with the sermon.

A newer and more popular phrase is "to communicate" the sermon. The word communicate means "to impart, to share, to distribute, to hold in common, to give and receive." The idea is that the speaker shares his message with the listeners; he transmits it to them so that they take hold of it and possess it. To communicate means more than to make the people hear the sermon, or be interested in it, or to understand it—it involves receiving it, considering it, and responding either negatively or positively to it. This concept involves the audience in the preaching process as well as the preacher and his sermon.

The responsibility to communicate is taken seriously by the secular world today. Universities, businesses, governments and religious organizations have departments of

133

communication. Churches and preachers need to think about it.

Our interest centers on communicating the expository sermon, though most of what we say applies to other types of sermons too. All of the essentials discussed in previous chapters help in communication. In other words, if the explanation is sound, the organization clear, the argumentation strong, the illustrations appropriate, the application pointed, and the imagination active, the sermon has gone a long way toward communication. However, there are other items to be considered.

The preacher should be able to feel the pulse and sense the mood of the age in which he lives. To do this, he must be in touch with the currents of life and thought. Such understanding will help him slant his preaching to today's world rather than to yesterday's. Luccock says that ours is an age with a sense of insignificance, insecurity, anxiety, futility, emptiness.[1] Others call it a bewildered age where we live in a moral vacuum. Objective, valid moral standards are almost a thing of the past. What an age in which to preach the eternally fixed moral truths of divine revelation as revealed in expository preaching!

F. W. Dillistone of England raises this question: "How can a culture whose whole attention is focused upon the factual, the observable, the verifiable, the workable, suddenly turn aside to consider the unseen, the personal, the ethical, the eternal?"[2]

We believe that the expository preacher has the answer if anyone does.

William Faulkner, the novelist, came near the truth, when he said: "The young man or woman writing today has forgotten the problems of the human heart in conflict with itself which alone can make good writing because only that is worth writing about. . . . There should be room

134

in the writer's heart . . . only for the old verities and truths of heart, the old universal truths lacking which any story is ephemeral and doomed—love and honor and pity and pride and compassion and sacrifice."[3]

Faulkner was right on the human level, but the expository preacher rises to the higher level of the old universal truths of sin, sorrow, death, grace, redemption, love and service. But these eternally valid truths of divine revelation have to be related to the human predicament of today.

David H. C. Read has written: "The line of communication has been cut; and there is no real contact between pulpit and pew. Sad though it may sometimes seem to us in our dreams of the ideal sermon, conceived in quietness and delivered without complications, it remains an axiom of Christian preaching that the road from the study to the pulpit runs through a living, demanding, interrupting manse; out into the noisy street; in and out of house and hospitals, farms and factories, buses, trains, cinema; through ringing telephones and stacks of letters and minutes; up between rows of puzzled people to the place where you are called to preach. It cannot be otherwise. . . . This necessity of a living contact with the real world arises both from our situation *in* the world . . . and also from the very nature of the Word of God."[4]

The author's opinion is that some writers have overdrawn the picture of the present breakdown of communication between the pulpit and the pew. If the expository preacher is a pastoral caller and counseler, and is involved constructively in the affairs of his community, he will be in touch with life and able to communicate from the pulpit.

The expository preacher will wish to gain the backing and cooperation of his audience in his program of expository preaching. He can do this by showing them that he is preaching *for* them as well as *to* them. He is their mouth-piece. He speaks for the whole congregation, not merely for himself. His source of authority and preaching material is their Bible, the standard of their faith and practice. He is seeking to help them understand and live it. His sources of information about the Bible are standard helps recognized and approved by the whole church of Christ, not merely their own denomination. His interpretations are not offhand, personal ones, but they have been checked and tested by reliable Biblical authorities, and are, therefore, worthy of careful consideration. The preacher's congregation will appreciate and respond to this type of approach.

The preacher should invite his people to bring their Bibles to church and to look up his texts and references. Then he can invite them to share their reactions, opinions, and questions with him either in personal conversation or by telephone.

A good way to arouse the interest and cooperation of the congregation is to have them vote on themes for different preaching series: favorite Bible chapters, favorite Bible characters, favorite Bible books for exposition, and favorite texts.

H. H. Halley's *Bible Handbook* has a section entitled, "The Most Important Thing in This Book." It is a plan of congregational Bible reading from which the pastor takes his sermon each week, "thus connecting the pastor's preaching with the people's Bible reading. This suggestion, if followed, would, beyond any doubt whatever, produce a Re-Vitalized Church. . . ."[5] This plan would certainly create a great measure of cooperation between pastor and congregation, and ought to be followed more than it is.

The preacher must demonstrate "by kindly word and virtuous life" the message which he preaches. The Bible must be not only his source for sermons, but his source of spiritual life and strength. His attitudes, practices and

136

ethics must be those of Biblical Christianity. The people must be able to believe absolutely in his sincerity and personal holiness. Carlos Greenleaf Fuller wrote an article entitled, "How to Preach With Power," in which he described the preacher who led him to Christ when he was a boy of fifteen: "In daily life that modest preacher whom God used to open my eyes and heart to redemptive grace lived where Peter and Paul lived. . . . He lived daily in an abiding death and resurrection union with Christ. . . . Another apostolic element in that preacher's life was that he expounded Spirit-wielded Scripture. Though he had had training and learning, he made no effort to preach in the wisdom of man. The Bible was God's revelation, and since his own life was based on that unshakable conviction, he spoke in the pulpit with great humility and holy boldness . . . when he prayed, the Holy Spirit winged his words into my heart and gave me the great blessing that a young man can know. . . ."[6]

In preparing an expository sermon, the preacher should be enthusiastic about his discoveries. H. E. Luccock said, "One first indispensable equipment for communicating the truth in the Bible is a strong sense of the romance of exegesis . . . sound exegesis, so far from being a merely scholarly or scientific undertaking, can be a thrilling adventure in discovery."[7]

As the preacher puts his sermon into shape his enthusiasm should increase. As he continues his meditation and prayer over it, his enthusiasm should continue to mount until he can hardly wait until time to preach. In his pulpit presentation, he will communicate his enthusiasm as well as his message. How can the expository preacher fail to be enthusiastic? He speaks from the greatest Book ever written, and deals with the most important truths ever revealed.

The conversational style of delivery is in vogue today.

The speaker addresses the audience as if he were in private conversation with each person. This does not imply conversational volume and informality, but conversational directness. The former cultivated eloquence and soaring oratory is no more, except in rare instances. Listeners wish a speaker to say what he has to say in the most direct and interesting manner possible and be done with it. The conversational manner will give interest and warmth to the quality of the speaker's voice, enabling him to vary the volume, pitch, quality and rate of delivery. The expository preacher should be earnest, sincere, straightforward, natural, alert, and animated in delivery. If he cannot overcome bad speech faults such as nasality, throatiness, breathiness, raspiness, squeakiness, harshness, thinness, and monotones, he should seek the help of a qualified speech teacher. He should cultivate resonance, depth, and melodiousness so that it will be a pleasure to hear him speak.

The conversational preacher will maintain constant eye-contact with his listeners, glancing from one to another as his sermon proceeds. His gestures will be free and natural. They will express his feelings and ideas without excess. The conversational speaker will show deep respect for his audience, his message, and the Christian pulpit which he occupies. His pulpit attire should be modest, neat, appropriate and inconspicuous.

Style refers to the characteristic way one speaks or writes. It concerns the speaker's use of language and involves words, phrases, sentences, and paragraphs. Many ministers fail to communicate properly because they neglect style. They think that ideas are enough; the words will take care of themselves. Consequently their style is dull, abstract, and colorless. Broadus says the basic qualities of good sermon style are clarity, energy of language, and elegance. Phelps lists them as purity, precision, individual-

138

ity, perspicuity, energy, elegance and naturalness. Shedd enumerates them as plainness, force, beauty.

Because a sermon is a spoken message, the preacher should cultivate an oral style consisting of clear words, simple words, exact words, action words and picture words. He will do well to follow the example of J. H. Jowett who constantly studied words. Words are his stock in trade, and like G. Campbell Morgan, he should be the master of them.

For clarity and interest the *Reader's Digest* sets a splendid example. For vividness and accuracy, the weekly magazine, *Time*, can teach us a great deal. For beauty of style, couched in ancient terms, the King James Version of the Bible cannot be surpassed; but for beauty and accuracy of modern English, the Revised Standard Version sets a high standard. We recommend the books of Andrew W. Blackwood, a writer in the field of preaching and practical theology, whose style measures up to all desirable standards. He is simple, clear, accurate, elegant, and interesting. For one in the expository preaching field today, whose style leaves little to be desired, we point to Paul S. Rees. The best style draws least attention to itself. It conveys meaning without coloring or hindering it. Time invested in improving one's style is never wasted but will bring lifelong dividends.

The Holy Spirit is the divine Communicator. He communicated the Scriptures originally to holy men of God who recorded them under His inspiration. The Holy Spirit makes the written Word vital in human experience. One of the functions of the Spirit is to empower the preaching of the Word of God. Prophetic preaching was in the power of the Holy Spirit; the preaching of John the Baptist and of Jesus was in that power, and apostolic preaching was in the energy of the divine Spirit. Luke tells us of Jesus' preaching: "He opened the book and found the place where it was written, 'The Spirit of the Lord is upon me, because he has anointed me to preach good news to the poor, He has sent me to proclaim release to the captives and recovering of sight to the blind, to set at liberty those who are oppressed, to proclaim the acceptable year of the Lord' " (Luke 4:17-19, RSV).

If the expository preacher is to communicate his message effectively, he must do so in the power of the Holy Spirit. If he is to interpret Scripture correctly, discern its deeper meanings, quote it accurately, make it luminous, and apply it incisively, he will need the backing of the Holy Spirit.

The promise of the Spirit was connected with witnessing privately and publicly. Jesus said, "But you shall receive power when the Holy Spirit has come upon you; and you shall be my witnesses in Jerusalem and in all Judea and Samaria and to the end of the earth" (Acts 1:8, RSV).

Peter preached in the power of the Spirit: "Then Peter, filled with the Holy Spirit, said to them, 'Rulers of the people and elders . . .' " (Acts 4:8, RSV).

Paul preached in the power of the Holy Spirit when he wrote:

For I will not venture to speak of anything except what Christ has wrought through me to win obedience from the Gentiles, by word and deed, by the power of signs and wonders, by the power of the Holy Spirit, so that from Jerusalem and as far round as Illyricum I have fully preached the gospel of Christ . . . (Romans 15:18-19, RSV).

And I was with you in weakness and in much fear and trembling; and my speech and my message were not in plausible words of wisdom, but in demonstration of the Spirit and power, that your faith might not rest in the wisdom of men but in the power of God (I Corinthians 2:3-5, RSV).

. . . for our gospel came to you not only in word, but also in power and in the Holy Spirit and with full conviction. (I Thessalonians 1:5, rsv).

Peter said that the apostles were "those who preached the good news to you through the Holy Spirit sent from heaven . . ." (I Peter 1:12, rsv). How can we dare handle the Holy Scriptures in mere human wisdom and energy when the Holy Spirit is available to empower us? In spite of all the splendid modern translations of the Bible, the new lexical aids, and the great commentaries old and new, our preaching will fail to communicate the message and life of God if it depends solely on these and does not call on the power of the Holy Spirit.

A. J. Gordon, speaking of the decline in preaching, said: "And this decline is due, we believe, more than anything else, to an ignoring of the Holy Spirit as the supreme inspirer in preaching. We wish to see a great orator in the pulpit, forgetting that the least expounder of the Word, when filled with the Holy Ghost, is greater than he. . . . The true preacher does not simply use the Spirit; he is used by the Spirit. He speaks as one moving in the element and atmosphere of the Holy Ghost, and mastered by his divine power."[8]

F. B. Meyer believed that the expository preacher had a right to expect the cooperation of the Holy Spirit in handling sacred truth. He wrote: "But—and this is the most pertinent point for our present purpose, the Holy Spirit's power proceeds along the line of the Word of God, as the electric message along the wires. It is His sword; the lifegiving seed which He has vitalized; the word in which the Word is incarnated. Through long centuries He has been at work communicating to prepared natures the thoughts of God, and naturally He avails Himself of His prerogative. The ministry, therefore, which is most carefully based on

141

Scripture and honors Scripture and saturates itself with Scripture is the ministry which the Spirit of Truth can co-operate with in the most perfect abandonment."[9]

G. Campbell Morgan believed essentially the same thing. He wrote: "No man can do the work of God until he has the Holy Spirit, and is endued with power. It is impossible to preach the gospel save in the power of the Spirit, because none can comprehend the true meaning of the Cross of Christ unless taught by the Spirit of God. Neither a knowledge of the letter of the New Testament nor a system of theology, is sufficient to equip for preaching the cross. Nothing short of the immediate, direct, personal illumination of the Spirit is sufficient equipment."[10]

Alexander Maclaren believed in and labored in the power of the Holy Spirit. Speaking on Luke 24:49, "And, behold, I send the promise of my Father upon you . . .," he said: "The equipment for work is investiture with divine power. A partial bestowment of the Spirit, which is the Father's promise, took place while Jesus spoke. 'I send' refers to something done at the moment; but the fuller clothing with that garment of power was to be waited for in expectancy and desire. No man can do the Christian work of witnessing for and of Christ without that clothing with power. It was granted as an abiding gift on Pentecost. It needs perpetual renewal. We may all have it. Without it, eloquence, learning, and all else, are but as sounding brass and a tinkling cymbal."[11]

The preacher's temptation is to trust himself and his preparation rather than the Holy Spirit. With that attitude he never realizes the power of the Spirit in his preaching. Alan Redpath put it this way: "When our confidence is in gimmicks, programs, schemes, and planning, and we have not learned to seek first the Lord in the power of the Holy Spirit, in brokenness at Calvary, we inevitably go on being defeated and losing the battle."[12]

142

We must also recognize that preaching the Word of God, from the New Testament point of view, involves supernatural forces. Human minds are supernaturally darkened by sin and perverted by selfishness. Satanic powers resist the entrance of light through the Word of God. Paul said,

In their case the god of this world has blinded the minds of the unbelievers, to keep them from seeing the light of the gospel of the glory of Christ, who is the likeness of God (II Corinthians 4:4, RSV).

. . . when you were dead through the trespasses and sins in which you once walked, following the course of this world, following the prince of the power of the air, the spirit that is now at work in the sons of disobedience (Ephesians 2:1-2, RSV).

The sum total of natural abilities and acquired skills is not enough to communicate the saving gospel under such conditions. Even in the case of Christians, we encounter carnality and dullness enough to hinder communication unless we preach in the power of the Spirit. Paul expressed it this way:

But I, brethren, could not address you as spiritual men, but as men of the flesh, as babes in Christ. I fed you with milk, not solid food; for you were not ready for it; and even yet you are not ready, for you are still of the flesh (I Corinthians 3:1-2, RSV).

About this we have much to say which is hard to explain, since you have become dull of hearing. For though by this time you ought to be teachers, you need some one to teach you again the first principles of God's word. You need milk, not solid food . . . (Hebrews 5:11-12, RSV).

Only as preachers proclaim the Word of God in the power of the Holy Spirit can the living Word step forth in supernatural strength to break through these communication barriers. The writer to the Hebrews expressed it in these words: "For the word of God is living and active, sharper than any two-edged sword, piercing to the division of soul and spirit, of joints and marrow, and discerning the thoughts and intentions of the heart. And before him no creature is hidden, but all are open and laid bare to the eyes of him with whom we have to do" (Hebrews 4:12-13, RSV).

The man in the pulpit could be a false prophet instead of the true prophet he thinks he is. If he speaks without supernatural enduement, the words of H. Grady Davis could be true of him: "He comes speaking in the name of the Lord, but the Lord may have no control over him and no influence on what he says . . . he may have no notion who the Holy Spirit is. . . . He may be a false prophet."[13]

What can we expect the Holy Spirit to do in and through us in expository preaching? He can guide us in choosing the right Scripture passages for each occasion; guide us in the selection of books to buy and use in studying the Bible; give us illumination and insight in studying the passage; aid our memory to recall parallel passages and fitting illustrations; give us joy in concentrating on the text and the strength to push through the writing or verbalizing of the sermon; give us boldness and confidence at the time of delivery; inspire us with new thoughts during delivery and cause us to omit less appropriate ones. He can unify the audience, create attentiveness, open hearts, and apply the Word in both expected and unexpected ways. The Holy Spirit can convict, convert, comfort, inspire, reprove, correct, and instruct in righteousness. He can fix the Word in the minds and memories of hearers so that it becomes fruitful like the seed on good soil. How foolish to try to prepare sermons and preach them apart from the power of the Spirit!

How can the pastor assure himself that he will be preaching in the power of the Holy Spirit and not merely in the energy of the flesh? Perhaps there is no infallible way. We know so little about ourselves and our motives on the one hand, and so little about the deep things of the Spirit on the other, that it is unlikely we could lay out a formula and say, "If I follow this, I shall be certain to preach in the power of the Holy Spirit." Unknown to us, pride, selfishness, worldliness, or laziness can creep in and obstruct the way to power.

A few general observations ought to be in order, assuming that preparation has been done as recommended:

The preacher must be born again and know that he is truly a converted man, with sins forgiven and possessing sonship in the family of God, if he would preach in the Spirit's power.

He must live a clean life and be utterly sincere about his call and commitment to the ministry. The many hard conditions and vexations of the pastoral calling should not tempt him to seek some other line of work.

He must pursue depth studies in the Bible. He should be immersed in the Word of God as a daily practice, exploring, absorbing, using and memorizing it.

He must be absolutely obedient to the Lord. He cannot compromise or divide allegiance. "But if we walk in the light, as he is in the light, we have fellowship one with another, and the blood of Jesus his Son cleanseth us from all sin" (I John 1:7, KJV).

Another condition for preaching in the power of the Holy Spirit is a life of prayer. Power in preaching and pastoral work will normally be in direct proportion to the amount of time spent in prayer. We never have time to pray unless we make it. In times of prayer and waiting on God, the Spirit can come to us in His gracious ministry of teaching, guiding, comforting and strengthening.

Personal witnessing must be a practice if we would know the power of the Spirit. God gives the Spirit for the purpose of witnessing to Christ (Acts 1:8) and He honors those who witness by giving them more of the Spirit. Personal witnessing to individuals will keep us fresh, fragrant and fruitful. Its spiritual impact carries over into preaching.

A Survey on the Holy Spirit in Preaching

In 1950 one of the author's graduate students made a survey of the problem of the work of the Holy Spirit in preaching.[14] He sent out 102 questionnaires to leading evangelical ministers in the United States and Canada, and received sixty-two letters in reply. The questions he asked and a tabulation of the answers received are given below:

1. Can present-day preachers preach in the power of the Holy Spirit in the same degree as did the prophets and apostles?

   ANSWERS: Yes_____ 40
               Yes with qualifications_____ 20
               No answer _____ 2

2. When you preach, do you know whether or not you are preaching in the power of the Holy Spirit? How?

   ANSWERS: Yes_____ 38
               Yes with qualifications 16
               Doubtful _____ 2
               No _____ 2

The "How" part of this question was answered as follows:

3. In your experience, what are the prerequisites for preaching in the power of the Holy Spirit?

Several individual answers were also given.

4. What differences, if any, are there between preaching in the power of the Holy Spirit and any preaching that utilizes thorough preparation, personal magnetism, good psychology and rhetorical persuasion?

5. In your experience, what are the practical results of preaching in the power of the Holy Spirit?

Several individual answers were also given.

We can see that the goal of preaching in the power of the Holy Spirit is one that every preacher should have constantly before him. Apart from this experience, he really cannot communicate the gospel of Christ. Preaching in the power of the Holy Spirit is not a once-for-all experience that one attains and is thereafter certain of. It depends upon a continued life of spiritual growth and dedication, and must be sought separately for each and every preaching opportunity. A praying congregation can help a preacher of the Word to realize this goal.

Communicating the gospel is the greatest of all privileges that God gives to mortal man. The expository preacher has more of the gospel to communicate because he preaches from larger portions of the Bible, and he

148

preaches each portion in greater depth than the topical and textual preachers. Other qualifications being equal, he has a right to claim more power from the Holy Spirit in his preaching.

Notes

PREFACE

1. William M. Taylor, *The Ministry of the Word* (London, T. Nelson and Sons, 1876), p. 155.
2. F. B. Meyer, *Expository Preaching Plans and Methods* (New York, George H. Doran Co., 1912), p. 29.
3. Charles R. Brown, *The Art Of Preaching* (New York, The Macmillan Co., 1922), pp. 53-54.
4. Andrew W. Blackwood, *Expository Preaching for Today* (New York, Abingdon-Cokesbury Press, 1953), p. 13.
5. Ilion T. Jones, *Principles and Practice of Preaching* (Chicago, Moody Press, 1952), p. 59.
6. Douglas M. White, *He Expounded* (Chicago, Moody Press, 1952), p. 59.
7. T. H. Pattison, *The Making of the Sermon,* revised (Philadelphia, American Baptist Publication Society, 1941), p. 53.
8. M. Reu, *Homiletics* (Augsburg Publishing Co., 1924), p. 428.
9. P. T. Forsyth, *Positive Preaching and the Modern Mind* (New York, Hodder & Stoughton, 1907), p. 166.
10. John A. Broadus, *A Treatise on the Preparation and Delivery of Sermons* (Philadelphia, Smith, English & Co., 1876), p. 303.
11. Austin Phelps, *Theory of Preaching* (New York, Charles Scribner's Sons, 1887), pp. 21 and 32.
12. H. Jeffs, *The Art of Exposition* (London, James Clarke, 1910), p. 9.
13. R. Ames Montgomery, *Expository Preaching* (Westwood, N. J., Fleming H. Revell Co., 1939), p. 42.
14. Clarence S. Roddy, *We Prepare and Preach* (Chicago, Moody Press, 1959), p. 29.
15. John Hall, *God's Word Through Preaching* (New York, Dodd Mead & Co., 1875), p. 71.
16. David R. Breed, *Preparing to Preach* (New York, George H. Doran Co., 1911), p. 387.
17. Jeff D. Ray, *Expository Preaching* (Grand Rapids, Zondervan Publishing House, 1940), pp. 71, 72.
18. G. Campbell Morgan, *Preaching* (Westwood, N. J., Fleming H. Revell Co., 1937), pp. 56-57.

19. Merrill F. Unger, *Principles of Expository Preaching* (Grand Rapids, Zondervan Publishing House, 1955), p. 33.
20. *Ibid.*, p. 48.
21. David Martyn Lloyd-Jones, *Studies in the Sermon on the Mount*, Vol. I (Grand Rapids, Wm. B. Eerdmans Publishing Co., 1959), p. vii.
22. Donald G. Miller, *The Way to Biblical Preaching* (New York, Abingdon-Cokesbury Press, 1957), pp. 22-24.

CHAPTER I
1. William M. Taylor, *The Ministry of the Word* (London, T. Nelson and Sons, 1876), p. 29.
2. H. Jeffs, *The Art of Exposition* (London, James Clarke, 1910), p. 21.
3. Jill Morgan, *A Man of the Word* (Westwood, N. J., Fleming H. Revell Co., 1951), pp. 39-40.
4. Billy Graham, "Biblical Authority in Evangelism," *Christianity Today*, Vol. I, No. 1 (October 15, 1955), pp. 5-7.
5. Walter P. Doe, *Effective Revival Preaching* (Providence, A. Crawford Green, 1876), p. 171.
6. F. B. Meyer, *Expository Preaching Plans and Methods* (New York, George H. Doran Co., 1912), pp. 103, 106.
7. Joseph Parker, *These Sayings of Mine* (New York, Funk & Wagnalls, 1881), p. vii.
8. Harold J. Ockenga, *Every One That Believeth* (Westwood, N. J., Fleming H. Revell Co., 1942), p. 7.
9. R. Ames Montgomery, *Expository Preaching* (Westwood, N. J., Fleming H. Revell Co., 1939), p. 75.
10. Ernest Ruark, "Preach the Word," *The Watchman Examiner* (February 12, 1948), p. 155.
11. Bernard Ramm, "Expository Preaching," *The Watchman Examiner* (June 26, 1947), pp. 656-57.
12. *Ibid.*, p. 656.
13. Adolph Saphir, *The Epistle to the Hebrews*, Vol. I (New York, Christian Alliance Publishing Co., n.d.), p. 303.

CHAPTER II
1. Clarence S. Roddy, *We Prepare and Preach* (Chicago, Moody Press, 1959), p. 115.
2. *Ibid.*, p. 162.
3. *Ibid.*, p. 33.
4. M. Reu, *Homiletics* (Minneapolis, Augsburg Publishing Co., 1924), p. 319.

5. Paul S. Rees, *The Adequate Man* (Westwood, N. J., Fleming H. Revell Co., 1959), p. 7.

6. Jeff D. Ray, *Expository Preaching* (Grand Rapids, Zondervan Publishing House, 1940), pp. 59, 68.

7. H. Jeffs, *The Art of Exposition* (London, James H. Clarke, 1910), pp. 102-134.

8. Andrew W. Blackwood, *Preaching from the Bible* (New York, Abingdon-Cokesbury Press, 1941).

9. Harry C. Mark, *Patterns for Preaching* (Grand Rapids, Zondervan Publishing House, 1959), pp. 143-178.

10. L. M. Perry and F. D. Whitesell, *Variety in Your Preaching* (Westwood, N. J., Fleming H. Revell Co., 1954), pp. 34-43.

11. Chalmer E. Faws, *A Guide to Biblical Preaching* (Nashville, Broadman Press, 1962).

12. E. C. Dargan, *A History of Preaching*, Vol. II (New York, George H. Doran Co., 1912), pp. 575-77. (Reprinted by permission Baker Book House, Grand Rapids, 1954).

13. Alexander Maclaren, *Expositions of Holy Scripture*, Vol. IX (Grand Rapids, Wm. B. Eerdmans Publishing Co., 1952), quoted on inside cover back page.

14. A. W. Blackwood, *Expository Preaching for Today* (New York, Abingdon-Cokesbury Press, 1953), pp. 18-19.

15. G. Campbell Morgan, *The Westminster Pulpit*, Vol. I (Westwood, N. J., Fleming H. Revell Co., 1955), p. 7.

16. Don M. Wagner, *The Expository Method of G. Campbell Morgan* (Westwood, N. J., Fleming H. Revell Co., 1957), p. 69.

17. James R. Blackwood, *The Soul of Frederick W. Robertson* (New York, Harper and Brothers, 1947), Introduction, p. ix.

18. E. C. Dargan, *op. cit.*, p. 523.

19. James R. Blackwood, *op. cit.*, p. 105.

20. *Ibid.*, pp. 106, 110.

21. E. C. Dargan, *op. cit.*, p. 523.

22. F. R. Webber, *A History of Preaching in Britain and America*, Vol. I (Milwaukee, Northwestern Publishing House, 1952), p. 546.

23. Joseph Parker, *These Sayings of Mine* (New York, Funk & Wagnalls, 1881), p. 7.

24. Alexander Gammie, *Preachers I Have Heard* (London, Pickering and Inglis, Ltd., 1945), p. 40.

25. A. Chester Mann, *F. B. Meyer, Preacher, Teacher, Man of God* (Westwood, N. J., Fleming H. Revell Co., 1929), p. 29.

26. Alexander Gammie, *op. cit.*, p. 135.

27. F. B. Meyer, *Great Pulpit Masters*, Vol. VI (Westwood, N.J., Fleming H. Revell Co., 1950), introduction pp. 7-8.

28. Donald G. Barnhouse, *Man's Ruin* Romans, Vol. I (Wheaton, VanKampen Press, 1952), p. 12.
29. Paul S. Rees, *op. cit.,* p. 7.
30. Roy L. Laurin, *Where Life Endures* (Findlay, Ohio, Dunham Publishing Co., 1946).
31. Edgar DeWitt Jones, *The Royalty of the Pulpit* (New York, Harper & Brothers, 1951), p. 123.
32. W. H. Griffith Thomas, *The Work of the Ministry* (New York, Hodder & Stoughton, n.d.), pp. 229-30.

CHAPTER III
1. William Barclay, *The Gospel of Luke* (Philadelphia, Westminster Press, 1952), p. 230.
2. Alexander Whyte, *Bible Characters, Our Lord's Characters* (Edinburgh and London, Oliphants Ltd., n.d.), p. 87.
3. George A. Buttrick, *The Interpreter's Bible,* Luke, Vol. VIII (New York, Abingdon-Cokesbury Press, 1952), p. 306.
4. C. P. Eiselen, Edwin Lewis, and D. G. Downey, *The Abingdon Bible Commentary* (New York, Abingdon-Cokesbury Press, 1929), p. 1051.
5. Norvall Geldenhuys, *New International Commentary on the New Testament* (Grand Rapids, Wm. B. Eerdman's Publishing Co., 1951), p. 1951.
6. George A. Buttrick, *The Parables of Jesus* (New York, Doubleday, Doran & Co., 1929), pp. 166-175.
7. William M. Taylor, *The Parables of Our Saviour* (New York, Doubleday, Doran & Co., 1929), p. 416.
8. G. Campbell Morgan, *The Gospel According to Luke* (Westwood, N. J., Fleming H. Revell Co., 1931), pp. 202-203.
9. J. C. Ryle, *Expository Thoughts on the Gospels,* Luke, Vol. II (Grand Rapids, Zondervan Publishing House, n.d.), p. 252.
10. Alexander Whyte, *op. cit.,* p. 88.
11. Francis Davidson, *The New Bible Commentary* (Grand Rapids, Wm. B. Eerdmans Publishing Co., 1953), p. 857.
12. James Hastings, *The Speaker's Bible,* St. Luke, Vol. III (Aberdeen, Scotland, The Speaker's Bible Offices, 1926), p. 146.
13. George A. Buttrick, *op. cit.,* p. 169.

CHAPTER IV
1. G. Campbell Morgan, *Preaching* (Westwood, N. J., Fleming H. Revell Co., 1937), pp. 60-61, 70.
2. Halford E. Luccock, *In the Minister's Workshop* (New York, Abingdon-Cokesbury Press, 1944), p. 118.
3. Clarence S. Roddy, *We Prepare and Preach* (Chicago, Moody Press, 1959), p. 118.

4. Ilion T. Jones, *Principles and Practice of Preaching* (New York, Abingdon-Cokesbury Press, 1956), pp. 93-99.
5. Donald Macleod, *Here is My Method* (Westwood, N. J., Fleming H. Revell Co., 1952), p. 126.
6. F. D. Whitesell, *Expository Sermon Outlines* (Westwood, N. J., Fleming H. Revell Co., 1959), pp. 7-8.
7. W. H. Griffith Thomas, *St. Paul's Epistle to the Romans* (Grand Rapids, Wm. B. Eerdmans Publishing Co., 1946), pp. 120-25.
8. Harold J. Ockenga, *Every One That Believeth* (Westwood, N. J., Fleming H. Revell Co., 1942), pp. 78-87.
9. William G. Coltman, *Galatians, the Grace Way of Life* (Findlay, Ohio, Dunham Publishing Co., 1955), pp. 54-64.
10. Alexander Maclaren, *Expositions of Holy Scripture,* Luke (New York, A. C. Armstrong & Son, 1909), pp. 132-37.
11. J. C. Ryle, *Expository Thoughts on the Gospels,* Luke, Vol. II (Grand Rapids, Zondervan Publishing House, n.d.), pp. 252-256.
12. George A. Buttrick, *The Parables of Jesus* (New York, Doubleday Doran & Co., 1929), pp. 107-175.
13. W. B. Riley, *The Bible of the Expositor and the Evangelist,* New Testament Vol. IV (Cleveland, Union Gospel Press, 1926), pp. 147-164.
14. H. D. M. Spence and Joseph H. Excell, *The Pulpit Commentary,* Vol. XVI (Grand Rapids, Wm. B. Eerdmans Publishing Co., 1950), p. 115.
15. J. Willock, *The Preacher's Complete Homiletic Commentary on the New Testament,* Luke (New York, Funk & Wagnalls Co., n.d.), pp. 480-86.
16. *Ibid.,* p. 484.
17. *Ibid.,* p. 486.
18. Charles H. Spurgeon, *The Treasury of the New Testament* (Grand Rapids, Zondervan Publishing House, 1950), pp. 68-73.
19. F. D. Whitesell, *Expository Sermon Outlines* (Westwood, N. J., Fleming H. Revell Co., 1959), p. 39.
20. F. D. Whitesell, *Sermon Outlines on Women of the Bible* (Westwood, N. J., Fleming H. Revell Co., 1962), p. 52.
21. Walter T. Conner, *The Epistles of John* (Westwood, N. J., Fleming H. Revell Co., 1929), pp. 141-161.
22. *Ibid.,* pp. 162-174.
23. Charles Simeon, *Horae Homileticae,* Vol. XVIII (London, Samuel Holdsworth, 1838), pp. 334-346.
24. *Ibid.,* pp. 153-156.
25. F. D. Whitesell, *Sermon Outlines on Favorite Bible Chapters* (Westwood, N. J., Fleming H. Revell Co., 1962), p. 56.
26. V. L. Stansfield, *Favorite Sermons of John A. Broadus* (New York, Harper & Brothers, 1959), pp. 14-20.

155

CHAPTER V

1. David R. Breed, *Preparing to Preach* (New York, George H. Doran Co., 1911), p. 219.
2. *Ibid.*, pp. 221-222.
3. T. H. Pattison, *The Making of the Sermon*, revised (Philadelphia, American Baptists Publication Society, 1941), p. 225.
4. Phillips Brooks, *Lectures on Preaching* (New York, E. P. Dutton & Co., 1877), p. 110.
5. V. L. Stansfield, *Favorite Sermons of John A. Broadus* (New York, Harper & Brothers, 1959), p. 160.
6. *Ibid.*, p. 185.
7. *Ibid.*, p. 161.
8. James H. McBurney, James M. O'Neill, and Glen E. Mills, *Argumentation and Debate* (New York, Macmillan Company, 1951), pp. 210-213.
9. L. M. Perry and F. D. Whitesell, *Variety in Your Preaching* (Westwood, N. J., Fleming H. Revell, Co., 1954), pp. 25-26.
10. Alan H. Monroe, *Principles and Types of Speech* (Chicago, Scott, Foresman & Co., 1955), pp. 317-328.
11. David R. Breed, *op. cit.*, pp. 228-229.
12. Walter A. Maier, *Let Us Return Unto the Lord* (St. Louis, Concordia Publishing House, 1947), pp. 37-52.
13. F. W. Robertson, *Sermons Preached at Brighton* (New York, Harper & Brothers, 1905), pp. 426-36.
14. *Ibid.*

CHAPTER VI

1. Donald G. Smith, *Sermon Illustration*, Th.M. thesis (Northern Baptist Theological Seminary, Chicago, 1951), pp. v, vi.
2. F. D. Whitesell, *Evangelistic Illustrations from the Bible* (Grand Rapids, Zondervan Publishing House, 1955), Foreword pp. 4-5.
3. Harry A. Ironside, *Addresses on the First Epistle to the Corinthians* (New York, Loizeaux Brothers, 1938), pp. 186-87.
4. J. H. Jowett, *The High Calling, Meditations on St. Paul's Letter to the Philippians* (Westwood, N. J., Fleming H. Revell Co., 1909), p. 29.
5. *Ibid.*, p. 17.
6. *Ibid.*, p. 20.
7. *Ibid.*, p. 21.
8. *Ibid.*, p. 26.
9. *Ibid.*, p. 30.
10. *Ibid.*, p. 39.
11. Marcus Dods, *The Gospel of St. John*, Vol. II (New York, George H. Doran Co., n.d.), p. 81.
12. *Ibid.*, p. 82.

13. *Ibid.*, p. 85.
14. W. B. Riley, *The Bible of the Expositor and the Evangelist,* New Testament, Vol. IV (Cleveland, Union Gospel Press, 1926), pp. 219-31.
15. J. D. Jones, *The Lord of Life and Death* (New York, George H. Doran Co., n.d.), p. 141.
16. Alexander Maclaren, *Expositions of Holy Scripture,* St. Luke (New York, A.C. Armstrong & Son, 1909), p. 143.
17. *Ibid.*, p. 143.
18. *Ibid.*, p. 146.
19. *Ibid.*, p. 147.
20. *Ibid.*, p. 150.
21. *Ibid.*, p. 151.
22. G. Campbell Morgan, *The Westminster Pulpit,* Vol. IX (Westwood, N. J., Fleming H. Revell Co., n.d.), pp. 65-66.
23. *Ibid.*, p. 66.
24. *Ibid.*, p. 99.
25. *Ibid.*, p. 101.
26. *Ibid.*, p. 103.
27. *Ibid.*, pp. 104-105.
28. *Ibid.*, p. 105.
29. *Ibid.*, p. 236.
30. F. B. Meyer, *Moses, the Servant of God* (Westwood, N. J., Fleming H. Revell Co., 1950), pp. 21-22.
31. *Ibid.*, p. 23.
32. *Ibid.*, pp. 39-40.
33. H. J. Ockenga, *The Church in God* (Westwood, N. J., Fleming H. Revell Co., 1956), p. 25.
34. *Ibid.*, p. 27.
35. *Ibid.*, p. 27.
36. *Ibid.*, p. 29.
37. *Ibid.*, p. 29.
38. *Ibid.*, p. 30.
39. *Ibid.*, p. 31.
40. *Ibid.*, p. 32.
41. *Ibid.*, p. 32.
42. *Ibid.*, p. 33.
43. *Ibid.*, p. 34.
44. *Ibid.*, p. 35.
45. *Ibid.*, p. 38.

CHAPTER VII
1. William Cleaver Wilkinson, *Modern Masters of Pulpit Discourse* (Philadelphia, The Judson Press, 1905), p. 88.

2. J. W. Etter, *The Preacher and His Sermon* (Dayton, Ohio, United Brethern Publishing House, 1891), pp. 371-372.
3. David R. Breed, *Preparing to Preach* (New York, George H. Doran Co., 1911), pp. 275-76.
4. Alexander Maclaren, *Expositions of Holy Scripture,* St. Luke (New York, A. C. Armstrong & Son, 1909), p. 134.
5. *Ibid.,* p. 136.
6. *Ibid.,* p. 137.
7. *Ibid.,* p. 138.
8. *Ibid.,* p. 139.
9. *Ibid.,* p. 140.
10. F. B. Meyer, *Moses, the Servant of God* (Westwood, N. J., Fleming H. Revell Co., 1950), p. 40.
11. *Ibid.,* p. 41.
12. *Ibid.,* p. 44.
13. *Ibid.,* p. 49.
14. *Ibid.,* p. 50.
15. G. Campbell Morgan, *The Westminster Pulpit,* Vol. IX (Westwood, N. J., Fleming H. Revell Co., 1950), p. 304.
16. *Ibid.,* p. 308.
17. *Ibid.,* p. 309.
18. *Ibid.,* p. 311.
19. *Ibid.,* p. 312.
20. *Ibid.,* p. 313.
21. Helmut Thielicke, *The Waiting Father,* Sermons on the Parables of Jesus (New York, Harper & Brothers, 1959), p. 42.
22. *Ibid.,* p. 44.
23. *Ibid.,* p. 48.
24. *Ibid.,* p. 49.
25. *Ibid.,* p. 50.
26. David R. Breed, *op. cit.,* p. 277.
27. Alexander Whyte, *Bible Characters,* First Series (London, Oliphants Ltd., n.d.), pp. 46-47.
28. *Ibid.,* p. 53.
29. J. B. Weatherspoon, *On the Preparation and Delivery of Sermons* (New York, Harper & Brothers, 1944), p. 211.
30. Harold J. Ockenga, *The Church in God* (Westwood, N. J., Fleming H. Revell Co., 1956), pp. 158-59.
31. T. DeWitt Talmage, *500 Selected Sermons,* Vol. XII (New York, The Christian Herald, 1900), p. 174.

CHAPTER VIII
1. M. Reu, *Homiletics* (Minneapolis, Augsburg Publishing Co., 1924), p. 193.

2. Daniel P. Kidder, *A Treatise on Homiletics* (New York, Nelson and Phillips, 1864), p. 139.
3. A. W. Blackwood, *Preaching from the Bible* (New York, Abingdon-Cokesbury Press, 1941), p. 199.
4. J. B. Weatherspoon, *On the Preparation and Delivery of Sermons* (New York, Harper & Brothers, 1944), p. 211.
5. Halford E. Luccock, *In the Minister's Workshop* (New York, Abingdon-Cokesbury Press, 1944), p. 112.
6. R. W. Dale, *Nine Lectures on Preaching* (London, Hodder and Stoughton, 1890), p. 48.
7. Walter Russell Bowie, *Preaching* (New York, Abingdon-Cokesbury Press, 1954), p. 195.
8. *Webster's New World Dictionary of the American Language*, College Edition (Cleveland & New York, The World Publishing Co., 1960), p. 723.
9. Alexander Maclaren, *Expositions of Holy Scripture*, St. Luke (New York, A. C. Armstrong & Son, 1909), p. 152.
10. *Ibid.*, p. 154.
11. *Ibid.*, p. 155.
12. *Ibid.*, p. 161.
13. G. Campbell Morgan, *The Westminster Pulpit* (Westwood, N. J., Fleming H. Revell Co., n.d.), p. 305.
14. *Ibid.*, p. 310.
15. *Ibid.*, p. 311.
16. *Ibid.*, p. 312.
17. D. L. Moody, *Bible Characters* (Grand Rapids, Zondervan Publishing House, 1952), p. 26.
18. T. DeWitt Talmage, *500 Selected Sermons*, Vol. XI (New York, The Christian Herald, 1900), p. 325.
19. Alexander Whyte, *Bible Characters*, 4th Series (London, Oliphants Ltd., n.d.), pp. 82-83.
20. *Ibid.*, 3rd Series, p. 189.
21. Clarence E. Macartney, *Greatest Men of the Bible* (New York, Abingdon-Cokesbury Press, 1941) p. 116.
22. Joseph Parker, *These Sayings of Mine*, Vol. XX (New York, Funk & Wagnalls, 1881), pp. 163-164.
23. *Ibid.*, p. 268.

CHAPTER IX
1. Clarence S. Roddy, *We Prepare and Preach* (Chicago, Moody Press, 1959), p. 168.
2. W. E. Sangster, *The Craft of Sermon Construction* (Philadelphia, Westminster Press, 1951), p. 176.

3. Ralph Sockman, *Look* Magazine (November 21, 1961, Vol. 25), p. 137.
4. Donald MacLeod, *Here is My Method* (Westwood, N. J., Fleming H. Revell Co., 1952), p. 72.
5. *Ibid.,* p. 95.
6. F. R. Webber, *A History of Preaching in Britain and America,* Part One (Milwaukee, Northwestern Publishing House, 1952), pp. 592-93.

CHAPTER X
1. Halford E. Luccock, *Communicating the Gospel* (New York, Harper & Brothers, 1954), pp. 77-79.
2. F. W. Dillistone, *Christianity and Communication* (New York, Charles Scribner's Sons, 1956), p. 15.
3. William Faulkner, *Chicago Daily News* (July 7, 1962), p. 5.
4. David H. C. Read, *The Communication of the Gospel* (London, SCM Press, Ltd., 1952), p. 63.
5. Henry H. Halley, *Bible Handbook,* 22nd edition (Grand Rapids, Zondervan Publishing House), p. 922.
6. Carlos G. Fuller, *Christianity Today* (Washington, D. C., January 5, 1959), p. 4.
7. Halford E. Luccock, *op. cit.,* p. 107.
8. A. J. Gordon, *The Ministry of the Spirit* (Philadelphia, American Baptist Publication Society, 1896), p. 145.
9. F. B. Meyer, *Expository Preaching Plans and Methods* (New York, George H. Doran Co., 1912), pp. 12-13.
10. G. Campbell Morgan, *The Spirit of God* (Westwood, N. J., Fleming H. Revell Co., 1900), pp. 203-204.
11. Alexander Maclaren, *Expositions of Holy Scripture,* St. Luke (New York, A. C. Armstrong & Son, 1909), p. 377.
12. Alan Redpath, *The Royal Route to Heaven* (Westwood, N. J., Fleming H. Revell Co., 1960), p. 36.
13. H. Grady Davis, *Design for Preaching* (Philadelphia, Muhlenberg Press, 1958), p. 91.
14. Raymond W. McLaughlin, *The Place of the Holy Spirit in Preaching,* Th.D. thesis (Northern Baptist Theological Seminary, Chicago, 1950), chapter V.

SERMON OUTLINE EXAMPLES

"The Praying Widow" (Luke 18:1-8)

I. Jesus regarded prayer as the simple outpouring of human need
II. Prayer must become a tireless beseeching before God can richly reward it
III. Our prayers must be freed of insincerity and the trivial spirit before heaven's bounty is unlocked
IV. Prayer is the central and determining force of a man's life

—Buttrick—

I. The great importance of perseverance in prayer
II. God has an elect people upon the earth who are under His special care
III. True faith will be found very scarce at the end of the world

—Ryle—

I. God in contrast with human avenger
II. God's people in contrast with the widow
III. The long-suffering of God in contrast with the long-suffering of man

—The Pulpit Commentary—

I. The wearisome widow and the unrighteous judge
II. The Pharisee and the publican

—Maclaren—

I. The helpless
II. The helper
III. The appeal
IV. The encouragements

—Wells—

I. Remarkable if we consider the person mentioned as searching for faith
   1. When Jesus comes He will look for precious faith
   2. He will do so in His most sympathetic character
   3. The Son of man is the most likely person to discover faith if it is to be found
   4. Faith always looks to Christ
   5. The Son of man will give a wise and generous judgment in the matter
   6. Notice the time of scrutiny
   7. Notice the breadth of the region of search
II. It is exceedingly instructive in connection with the parable of which it is a part
   1. When the Son of man comes, shall He find upon earth the faith which prays importunately as this widow did?
   2. The importunate widow wailed with strong resolve, and never ceased through sullen doubt
   3. The widow staked her all upon the result of her pleading with the judge
III. Our text is suggestive in view of its form
   1. It warns us not to dogmatize about what the latter days will be
   2. This question leads us to much holy fear as to the matter of faith
   3. Many processes are in vigorous action which tend to destroy faith
   4. In addition, are there not influences which dwarf and stunt faith?
   5. Does not this invite us to intense watchfulness over ourselves?
IV. My text is very impressive in respect to personal duty
   1. Let faith have a home in our hearts
   2. Hold on to the Holy Scriptures as a great source of faith
   3. Make certain that you are born of the Holy Spirit, for you cannot have faith otherwise
   4. Believe in the precious blood of Christ shed for your sins

5. Never relax your confidence in the efficacy of prayer, for the widow used no other weapon than prayer in her importunity with the judge
6. Believe up to the hilt. Plunge into this sea of holy confidence in God and you shall find waters to swim in

—Spurgeon—

I. The certainty of the Second Coming
II. The occasion of the Second Coming
III. The query concerning the Second Coming

—Riley—

I. Sense of need
II. Desire to get
III. Belief that God has in store what we desire
IV. Belief that though He withholds awhile, He loves to be asked
V. Belief that asking will obtain

—Arnot—

I. God always hears the true prayer
II. The reason of God's delay may be to increase our earnestness
III. Many prayers are never answered because men faint at God's delay

—Miller—

Our passage reveals four reasons for praying always.
I. Our Lord urged it, v. 1
  1. This is reason enough for true believers.
  2. Jesus Himself practiced it.
  3. It can be done if we try.
II. Life's emergencies require it, vv. 2-5
  1. This widow faced a real crisis.
  2. She prayed always to a wicked judge.
  3. Emergencies requiring prayer come to us, to our loved ones, to friends.

163

III. God's mercies encourage it, vv. 6-8
   1. Our God is the opposite of the wicked judge. He hears their cries.
   2. He is just and long-suffering.
IV. Son of man's return seeks it, v. 8
   1. When Christ returns He will seek the faith that prays always.
   2. He will render full and speedy justice.
   3. Will He find "the faith" in you?

Conclusion: Make prayer the unbroken habit and major force in your life. When we faint instead of praying, prayer becomes a farce instead of a force.

—Whitesell—

Index

Index

Index to Scriptures

Index to Scriptures